NARENDRA MODI

AND

NAGA PEACE ACCORD

BY OKEN JEET SANDHAM

SANDHAM NETWORK

First published by **Sandham Network in 2015, PO Box 583, Kohima 797 001, Nagaland, India.**

www.sandhamnetwork.in

Cover design by Reagan Kenye Sandham and Elizabeth Kenye Sandham

2

For

Aneile Kenye

TABLE OF CONTENTS

ACKNOWLEDGMENTS

I am thankful to many friends who have been encouraging me to write a book on the Naga issue. I am lucky to be a journalist. I had come across many great Naga political leaders and most of them are no more today. They are late JB Jasokie, late Dr Hokishe Sema, late Vizol and late Vamuzo --- all of them served as Chief Minister of Nagaland. I am privileged that I had interviewed all of them when they were alive. I also interviewed Dr SC Jamir, Governor of Odisha and former Nagaland Chief Minister; KL Chishi, former Nagaland Chief Minister; Neiphiu Rio, MP and former Nagaland Chief Minister; TR Zeliang, current Chief Minister of Nagaland; Dr Shurhozelie, President of Naga People's Front (NPF) and former Nagaland Minister and many Naga Ministers on many occasions. Honestly speaking, having sat and chatted with these great leaders and discussed the Naga political issue, I have really come to know not only the Naga history but also their magnanimity. And I used to think sometimes that the Indian leaders had really missed many opportunities to resolve the Naga political issue when things were not that complex. I am indebted to these great Naga leaders for sharing the issue that had confronted the Nagas for decades. I have also come across many Indian leaders including former Prime Ministers HD Deve Gowda, Atal Bihari Vajpayee, Dr Manmohan Singh, former

Deputy Prime Minister LK Advani, Ministers late Rajesh Pilot, Oscar Fernandez and George Fernandez. They all gave their best to resolve the Naga issue. I was also privileged to have interviewed top officials of India including GK Pillai and others like RS Pandey, former Interlocutor for Naga talks, Chairmen of Cease Fire Monitoring Group, etc. I have also come across leaders of various Naga civil societies, student bodies, church leaders and mothers, and grateful to them for sharing the crux of the Naga political issue. I am thankful to many leaders of the Naga nationalist groups who had openly shared the outcomes of various processes that had come along after the Government of India entered into the second ceasefire agreement with NSCN (IM) in 1997 and later with NSCN (K) in 2001. The first ever ceasefire was signed between the Government of India and the Federal Government of Nagaland (FGN) in 1964. I was so lucky that at least I was present at the grand funeral service of legendary Naga freedom fighter, AZ Phizo, held on May 11, 1990 at Kohima Local Ground. I was also lucky that I had interviewed Jwene, wife of AZ Phizo. Interviewing this great lady was a memorable one indeed. I was also lucky to have attended number of Press Conferences addressed by NSCN (IM) collective leaderships – Isak Chishi Swu and Th Muivah. I also interviewed many leaders of NSCN (K), some of them are now leaders of GPRN/NSCN (NSCN-KK), and leaders of FGN. I also exclusively interviewed Adino Phizo, President of

NNC and daughter of AZ Phizo. I am grateful to many Naga academics for sharing their past experiences with regard to the Naga political issue. I personally have high regard for the veteran Naga journalists - Mheisizokho Zinyu, late L Legiesie, Charles Chasie - who worked in worse times without compromising their professionalism. These great Naga journalists had inspired me a lot to become a journalist professionally and I am here today. I salute them today. I am indebted to my son, Reagan Kenye Sandham and daughter, Elizabeth Kenye Sandham for taking care of me particularly my health while I was heavily concentrating on writing the book. I personally thank Vishene, Priyanka, Mina, Sanathoibi (Naocha) and Memton who have been attending to my family, and their attending to us gave a huge relief but also helped me to complete the writing of the book. I owe a lot to my parents – Jilla Sandham and Radhe Sandham - who always encourage me to work for the downtrodden people. I thank all my in-laws who have been giving me all the comforts and peace without which I would not be able to concentrate on writing. I thank all my family members and relatives who have been providing me all the support while writing this book on the Naga issue. I thank all who have been cooperative throughout my writing.

Kohima   ***OKEN JEET SANDHAM***
3 December, 2015

FROM THE AUTHOR

History has shown us that many great freedom fighters took up arms to liberate from the occupational forces. Great leaders of India like Mahatama Gandhi, Netaji Subhas Chandra Bose, Jawaharal Nehru, Maulana Abul Kalam Azad, Bal Gangadhar Tilak, Sardar Vallabhbhai Patel, Gopal Krishna Gokhale, Dr. Rajendra Prasad, etc. fought vigorously against the British and many of them were put behind the bars for fighting against them (British occupational forces).

All Indians had a common "dream" and that was for a "Free India." Almost every one of them fought against the British in one way or the other to end the British imperialism in India. After a century of revolutions, struggles, battles and sacrifices, India finally achieved independence on 15 August 1947.

But the country lost countless men and women who were filled with undaunted courage and spirit of patriotism. Today, they are known as "freedom fighters" because they sacrificed their lives for their motherland.

Similarly many leaders in the Region including Bir Tikendrajit, Thangal General, Rani Gaidinliu, Haipo Jodonang, Gopinath Bordoloi, Piyoli Phukan, Phulguri Dhewa, Maniram Dewan, etc. too joined fighting against the British. Many of them were hanged to death for revolting against the British administration, while many had to languish in various jails in India.

Unfortunately, the British left this Indian sub-continent without settling many political issues and the Naga issue was one of it. The Naga leaders under the banner of Naga National Council (NNC) had boldly declared their "Independence" on 14 August 1947. The NNC leaders had done this after Indian leaders' unresponsive attitudes to their wanting to live as a free Nation. Whether one likes it or not, the decision of NNC leaders at that point of time in declaring the "Naga Independence" on 14 August 1947 became politically "historic and landmark." Till today, various Naga groups are observing the "Naga Independence Day" with great pride and honor. And the Government of India or for that matter the State Government of Nagaland has not prevented them so far from observing the "Naga Independence Day" in various Naga places.

Today, people may say many things of the Naga political struggle but if one looks back at the 50s, it is simply horrible. I had interacted with many Naga elders in many villages. Their stories were all the same. The Naga people had suffered enough at the hands of the Indian army. Most of the boys in the 50s could not go to schools for fear of being beaten or arrested by the India army, while males including teenage boys had to take shelter in jungles for days, weeks, months. Some were starved to death. All these horrendous acts were perpetrated on the innocent Naga villagers in the name of fighting Naga underground people. And the Nagas underwent all these unwanted just because they wanted to live as a free nation.

There were various occasions where many Naga leaders both overground and underground tried to solve the Naga political issue. Overground Naga leaders initiated process and even contacted NNC supremo, AZ Phizo at London. We have seen a series of correspondences between many Nagaland politicians including Dr SC Jamir and Phizo.

The emergence of Naga People's Convention (NPC) had changed the course of Naga history as they were responsible for the birth of a full-fledged Statehood of Nagaland in 1963. In the following year in 1964, ceasefire was declared between the Government of India and Federal Government of Nagaland (FGN) through the initiative of NBCC. Subsequently, talks were held for finding settlement to the Indo-Naga issue. The talks collapsed after six rounds. The problem remained and became more compounded as there were Naga leaders who ran the affairs of the Indian State of Nagaland needing to defend the "Sovereignty and Integrity of India." The Naga underground people became more aggressive and began fighting against their own people on the one hand and the Indian army on the other. The political process became trickier and riskier. Assassination of Naga leaders started, so also many abortive assassination attempts on Naga

15

politicians. The Naga underground leaders and the Naga overground people were at loggerheads over the Naga issue.

Then the Shillong Accord came in 1975. This Accord had done maximum damage to NNC. The immediate fallout of this Accord could be seen by the formation of another Naga underground group – National Socialist Council of Nagaland (NSCN) in 1980. After about a decade, the NSCN got split into two in 1988—one headed by Isak Chishi Swu and Th Muivah and the other by SS Khaplang and Dally Mungro. Following the split, hundreds of Naga underground cadres and high functionaries including Dally Mungro lost their precious lives due to factionalism. Sadly, it went on in large scale even after the Government of India's ceasefires with NSCN (IM) and NSCN (K). Many intellectuals and intelligentsias questioned the rationality of ceasefires with the Government of India. Some poised questions as to why Naga underground groups could not cease fighting amongst them when they could with Indian security forces. They also wondered on New Delhi's remaining as a mute spectator allowing factions to go free for all. This is where Naga civil societies came in to intervene.

Even after the DAN Government came into power in 2003, they set up committees to facilitate unity and reconciliation among the factions. In its second tenure, the DAN Government constituted Political Affairs Committee (PAC). Its members had extensively travelled and met leaders of various factions. They discussed the need of having unity and reconciliation among them. But everything seemed smooth till such time when the PAC mooted the idea of having a "Naga Common Platform." Members for Naga Common Platform would be drawn up from different political parties, NGOs, tribal hohos, etc. The basic premise of such arrangement was to evolve a consensus or majority opinion of the Naga people so as to endorse the Naga underground people to expedite talks with Delhi for an early solution to the Naga issue.

Unfortunately, PAC failed to function effectively following the formation of the Joint Legislators Working Group (JLWG). JLWC had overtaken the role of PAC.

On the other hand, Forum for Naga Reconciliation (FNR) also came into being in 2008 with renowned priest Rev Wati Aier as Convener. Since then, they had initiated "reconciliation" process for leaders of various Naga underground groups. They could succeed in breaking ice and further strengthen the journey of common hope. Who believed that members of NSCN factions would agree to meet each other and form a combined team to play soccer against combined team of different Naga NGOs. But the idea worked at last. It is a fantastic idea. These successive positive developments could pave way for top leaders of NSCNs and NNC/FGN to come and attend the "Highest Level Meeting" of leaders of Naga underground groups.

As far as the current status of the Naga political negotiation is concerned, solution to the extremely complicated Naga issue might come in anytime. The Government of India has already expressed "optimism" that solution to Naga issue will be arrived at soon.

Wanting freedom is not a crime. There is dignity in fighting for freedom and there is no any other dignified life other than being a freedom fighter.

Soon after Narendra Modi became the Prime Minister of India, the political pundits in the Northeast began to think that some kind of political solution to the Naga political issue might come soon. Because Modi's style of dealing with the Naga issue is different than his predecessors. He allows Interlocutor, RN Ravi, to take decision on the Naga issue, although the contents of the "Framework Agreement" signed between the Government of India and NSCN (IM) on 3 August 2015 at Delhi is yet to be known.

I have written this book mainly on the Prime Minister Modi's initiative to settle the Naga issue and thus named - "Narendra Modi and Naga Peace Accord."

I am lucky that I asked Atal Bihari Vajpayee on the Naga issue on two occasions – one at Shillong and the other at Kohima – when he was the Prime Minister. He had genuine love, care and concern for the Nagas, and this had won Nagas' hearts.

Yet, it appears that things are still not clear, though Naga leaders today appear to be "tolerant enough." It's a sign of maturity indeed as they cannot take any decision without seeing pros and cons, because the issue is seriously interlinked with many complicated issues.

What is lacking today in the leadership of the country is their "love, care, and concern" for the people of the Northeast. Wisdom and diplomacy is lacking in them. The solution is possible only when we understand each other and respect other's values, cultures, and traditions.

Prime Minister Modi must learn from Vajpayee, whose genuine love, care and concern for the Nagas changed the landscape of the Naga issue.

"I assure you that we will always be sensitive to the needs and concerns of the people of Nagaland, as also of the people of other North-Eastern States. Similarly, the people belonging to each State, and each ethnic group, in the North-East should be sensitive to the needs and concerns of their neighbors," Vajpayee said while attending the "First Convocation of Nagaland University" on 28 October 2003 at the Central Secretariat Plaza, Kohima. "Let us leave behind all the unfortunate things that happened in the past. For too long this fair land has been scarred and seared by violence. It has been bled by the orgy of the killings of human beings by human beings. Each death pains me. Each death diminishes us. My Government has been doing everything possible to stop this bloodshed, so that we can together inaugurate a new era of peace, development and prosperity in Nagaland."

CHAPTER ONE

MODI VISITED NAGALAND IN LESS THAN 7 MONTHS OF TAKING OVER PRIME MINISTERSHIP

Within seven months of assuming his office, Prime Minister Narendra Modi confirmed of his visiting Manipur and Nagaland to grace the Valedictory Celebration of the "Sangai Festival 2014" in Manipur and the Grand Opening Celebration of the "Hornbill Festival 2014" in Nagaland respectively. Manipur organizes the "Sangai Festival" annually from November 21 to 30 and Nagaland organizes the "Hornbill Festival" annually in the first week of December at Kisama, some 10 kilometers away from Kohima.

Initial doubts were Modi would not accept the invitation of Nagaland Chief Minister TR Zeliang to grace the Opening Celebration of the "Hornbill

Festival" on December 1, 2014. We doubted because he had just assumed his Office at Delhi only a few months back and had to sort out many things. But every one of us in the Northeast, particularly in Nagaland, was taken aback by his acceptance to visit Nagaland to grace the "Opening Ceremony of the Hornbill Festival 2014" at Kisama. In fact, when the Press people asked Zeliang whether he would be inviting the new Prime Minister to grace the upcoming "Hornbill Festival 2014 in Nagaland," he responded that they would definitely invite him but wasn't sure whether he would accept their invitation presuming he had just assumed his office a few months back.

Modi created unprecedented wave during the last Lok Sabha general elections across the country. He successfully marketed his State's "Gujarat Model" throughout the last Lok Sabha electioneering. Although we haven't seen any major States like UP, WB, Punjab, Rajasthan, Maharashtra and TN having enthusiasm in "Gujarat Model," his propagating "Gujarat Model" during electioneering continued to hog the limelight. It is also wondering whether the model, which was successful in one of the most advanced and industrialized States in the country, can be experimented in the Northeastern States of the country.

The Northeastern Region is the most neglected in all aspects of development. There is no industry or factory worth mentioning. Barring Assam and Tripura which are also struggling in many ways, the

State capitals of the Northeastern Region are yet to be connected with the railways. Many State capitals are still without airports. Most of the people in the Region are living in landlocked hilly terrains without basic infrastructures. And because of the lack of development and Center's near absence of their working systems with the respective State Governments in the Region, the social, political and economic conditions of the Region have become extremely pathetic and this development has given rooms for the neighboring countries to exploit to their advantages threatening to the peace and security of the Region and country well as.

The Ministry of Development of North Eastern Region (DoNER), established in September 2001, was basically to bridge the economic and developmental gap that had been between the Northeastern States of India and the rest of the country. There was initial euphoria over the creation of this Ministry but it didn't take long before it went into oblivion. It has been 14 years now that neither significant economic growth nor any policy for the economic development was seen. We only hear of earmarking 10% of their Annual Plan Budgets by the Central Ministries for the North Eastern Region to address the development deficit of the NER. Earmarking of 10% of the Annual Plan Budget of over 52 Ministries of the Union Government is immense. Yet, we hardly know how the money is spent.

In order to streamline, a serious review of the

functioning of the DonER Ministry is essential.

■■ ■■■ ■■■ ■■■ ■■■■

SOME OF THE URGENT STEPS TO BE TAKEN UP ARE:

The Office of the DoNER Ministry should be placed anywhere in the Northeast preferably at Shillong or Guwahati, instead of Delhi.

A nodal officer with minimum supportive staffs can be appointed and placed at each State Capital Headquarter of the Region. So that implementation of works can be expedited, besides it will minimize physical, financial and mental burdens on many. Citizens can also get proper access to the offices and get all the necessary information of the works under the Ministry meant for them.

The budgetary allocation for the DoNER Ministry, which is normally done on a lump sum, should be enhanced triple as the current allocation is too meager to take up any noticeable projects in the Region.

The DoNER Ministry should come up with modalities suitable for the Region's environment while constantly working on to incorporate the fundamental national character into the regional mainstream. This way the social fabric of national character remains.

North Eastern Council (NEC), which has its head office at Shillong, should be restructured and restored to its earlier model where any serving Governor of any State in the Region was Chairman. It was on a rotational basis. This system was, later, done away with. Now any DoNER Minister would automatically become the Chairman of the NEC and functions from Delhi. This way, the functioning of the NEC has been badly affected. NEC is normally considered as Regional Mini-Planning Commission and therefore, it is more appropriate going back to its earlier model by reappointing any senior serving Governor of any State in the Region as Chairman of it. In this way, the NEC can be effectively administered.

Nearly two lakh northeast youth majority of them are students have been staying in various major cities including Delhi for pursuing their higher studies, while others have been working in hotels, industries, factories, universities, colleges, etc.

It is illogical to demand everything to place in the Region to prevent the Northeastern youth and students from migrating to other cities to avoid racial attacks and segregations. But the fact is Northeast is least developed as already stated and one should agree that most of the Northeastern students who have gone to other parts of the country for pursuing their higher studies is largely due to lack of educational institutions with good infrastructures.

Sadly, there is not a single Medical College or Technical College or Engineering College in Nagaland even after 52 years of its Statehood. Is it the way to keep a State without a single Medical College? It is simply impossible for the educated youth of the State to compete with their counterparts in the rest of the country. The State is far behind in almost all the fields.

In fact, the Medical Colleges in the Region are not enough to accommodate students. The total Medical Colleges of the entire Northeastern Region are not even half of the number of Medical Colleges of Tamil Nadu State.

Four southern States account more than 41% of all the Medical Colleges in the country. Kerala, Karnataka, Andhra Pradesh and Tamil Nadu together have 159 of the country's 387 Medical Colleges (both government and private).

Very often, the policy makers and decision makers of the country tried to attribute the Region's backwardness to insurgency. But they failed to realize that the Center's chronic negligence caused imbalance, backwardness, and underdevelopment, hence the birth of many insurgents in the Region.

The Northeastern problem is not even 5 percent of those in UP, Gujarat, TN, WB. The moment you really start thinking to provide comprehensive connectivity, banking facilities, educational institutions with required infrastructures, factories, industries, improved health delivery systems, etc. to the Region, 80 percent of the region's problem will be solved. This will also be a natural answer to Region's insurgents.

The meeting of the 49th Annual Conference of Directors General of Police/Inspectors General of Police 2014 in Guwahati, first of its kind held in the Northeast Region in post-Indian Independence, is one right step Modi Government had initiated towards restoring national character in the mindsets of the Northeastern people, besides sending a positive message to the rest of the country.

Meetings of next DGPs and IGPs can be held at another Northeastern State capital and even other important meetings of the country can also be held in similar fashions. Let the rest of the country have soul-searching that Northeastern India is part and parcel of this great country.

The people of the Northeastern Region have suffered enough, most of them are not their creations, and they have high hope in Modi's leadership as PM of this country. It is heartening to note that the people from the Northeastern Region lit "Candles" across the country wherever they were on the day Modi took oath as the 15th Prime Minister of India at 6 PM on May 26, 2014. Their belief in him is "unique and history."

One can only imagine what kind of "Northeast India" it will be if he uses at least 5 percent out of $35 billion given to India by his Japanese counterpart Abe during his visit in Japan and another 5 percent from $100 billion given to India by Chinese President Xi Jinping during his visit in India, towards developing Northeastern Region.

But his statement that the Northeast cannot be developed from Delhi is well taken. "Is it possible to develop the Northeast while sitting in Delhi? No! Officials will visit and see how it is to be done," he said on his radio program 'Maan Ki Baat' on July 26, 2015. He said the Central teams would camp in various districts and villages in the Northeast and interact with people to know their problems.

Today's youth are more well-informed, educated, well-versed and they are not interested to live any more on the hollowness and rhetoric of politicians. They had clearly seen the weaknesses of Dr Manmohan Singh as the Prime Minister on many occasions.

On the other hand, they had seen the kind of leadership in Modi who knew how to keep today's youth close-knitted with his political strategies, visions and plans for the future of the country. Besides, they saw in Modi that he could take the country forward. At the same time, the Western countries as well as many powerful countries started appreciating his performances. He was thoroughly prepared for the game and most of the Congress veterans in the country were seen finding difficulties to face him. All these factors had given political edge to him.

Modi even knew the importance of the Northeastern Region and its people who have also been victims of a weak leadership of the country. They would also like to see someone who could really take care of their wellbeing. One should also realize that youths of the Region are equally concerned for their future. We are in 68 years of Independence and living in 21st Century. They also want to enjoy like others.

■ ■ ■ ■ ■ ■ ■ ■ ■ ■ ■ ■ ■ ■ ■ ■ ■ ■

THE POLITICAL UNCERTAINTY AND THE FATE OF NAGA POLITICAL ISSUE:

In the 10-year UPA regime, Dr. Singh and the NSCN (IM) had really narrowed down their differences. They could manage to remove political glitches. This is, without a doubt, a big achievement on their parts.

Out of the 16 years of peace process till 2013, the Congress-led UPA Governments had been dealing with the Naga underground leaders for 10 years. Dr. Singh used to say that the solution to the protracted Naga political issue would be arrived at during his tenure. It was, certainly, a welcome gesture. But in reality, since the nature of the process is political and when political stability is not there, no political talks can be safely held whatever the case may be. And the political instability in the Congress-led UPA Government had increased in their second tenure while their allies were heaping all the blames of the political crises on the weak leadership of the Government.

Yet, one should keep in mind that the UPA Government was a coalition one and the majority Congress alone could not take any political decision such as the Naga issue without the consent of their allies. Besides, the issue needs debating on the Floor of Parliament while consulting respective Chief Ministers of the Region. Because of this complicated process, a strong political will with a stable Government at the Center is needed.

On the other hand, present Nagaland MP, Neiphiu Rio was Chief Minister of Nagaland for eleven years since 2003 after defeating the powerful Congress regime of SC Jamir. He was at the helms of affairs for eleven years when the Government of India and the NSCN (IM) was completing 16 years of their peace process. But he kept saying that they were not a party to talks and acting only as a "facilitator" to the process.

■ ■ ■ ■ ■ ■ ■ ■ ■ ■ ■ ■ ■ ■ ■ ■ ■ ■

The people of Northeast saw Modi as one leader who would be able to push the slow pace of development of the Northeast to a fast pace. The Region's development is far behind comparing with the rest of the country.

The people in Nagaland wanted to see Modi and were very happy that he had readily accepted the invitation from Zeliang to grace the "Hornbill Festival 2014" at Kisama. Agreeing to visit Nagaland within a few months of assuming his office was significant in the history of post-India Independence, and also in view of the crucial ongoing Naga peace process.

There were tight securities in and around Kohima and Dimapur. There were temporary welcome gates erected along the road from Assam Rifles area to Kisama. He would be arriving from Imphal at Dimapur Airport on November 30, 2014, after attending the Valedictory Function of the Sangai Festival on November 30, 2014, at Imphal.

His Special Aircraft coming from Imphal touched down at the Dimapur Airport at about 6 PM, and he was received at the Airport by Nagaland Governor PB Acharya, Chief Minister Zeliang, MP Rio, Rajya Sabha MP Khekiho Zhimomi, Council of Ministers and other high-ranking officials. Hundreds of people standing on both sides of the road were waving to the Prime Minister as he was headed to Chumukedima Police Complex. He stayed overnight at Police Guest House, Chumukedima.

At the Chumukedima Police Complex, Modi met Governor Acharya and Chief Minister Zeliang. In the meeting, Zeliang apprised him of the State's precarious financial position and also submitted him a Memorandum for the development of the State and the early settlement of the Naga political issue.

Representatives of Naga Hoho, ENPO, Naga Council Dimapur, NBCC, ACAUT, NSF, NMA, Zeliangrong Heraka Association, Nagaland were among others who met the Prime Minister during his overnight stay at Chumukedima Police Complex. Representatives of Political Parties also met him.

The next day, he arrived at Kohima Assam Rifles Helipad by Chopper and from there he was going to Kisama by road to grace the Hornbill Festival 2014. Sections of people in the State wanted Modi to come by road from Dimapur to Kohima like Atal Bihari Vajpayee to experience State's road condition. Interestingly, when Vajpayee visited the State 12 years back and after experiencing bumpy rides from Dimapur to Kohima, he announced Rs 400 crore for four laning road construction of the Dimapur-Kohima sector of National Highway 29. But the mother climate made then NDA Prime Minister to cancel his Chopper trip to Kohima to experience road ride from Dimapur to Kohima. Thank God but regrettably, Modi's climate was different.

Already the venue of the Hornbill Festival at

Kisama was jam-packed. When Modi arrived at Kisama, Angamis in their colorful traditional attires were lining up on both sides of the road leading to the festival venue to welcome him. As soon as he entered the venue, cheers of his fans filled the venue. When he was about to climb up stairs to the dais, the VVIPs standing nearby – were introduced to him as Chief Ministers from neighboring Myanmar. They were U Thar Aye, Chief Minister of Sagaing Region and U Lajon Ngan Sai, Chief Minister of Kachin State. We from the gallery saw him talking to them. It was reported that Governor Acharya was slightly peeved as he was not pre-informed about the presence of two Myanmar Chief Ministers attending the grand "Opening Celebration of the Hornbill Festival 2014."

So many colorful traditional dances of Naga tribes and other communities were presented to Modi. He was attired with colorful Naga traditional dress including headgear, spear, and dao.

We were just sitting around 50 feet away from his dais anxiously waiting for his speech, so was everyone. When he was requested to address the mammoth gathering, the crowds cheered in joy.

Hopes were flying thick and high that he would say something special with regard to settlement of the protracted Naga political issue from Kisama. Thanking the Nagas for their hospitality and rich cultures, he spoke mostly for development of the

33

Region. He touched on the importance of developing tourism in the State for the economic boom.

Whatever Modi announced with regard to many schemes like Ishaan Uday; Ishaan Vikas; deciding to establish one modern apparel garment manufacturing center in every State of the North-East; Rs 28,000 crore for construction of 14 new railway lines; Rs 5,000 crore for power in six North-Eastern States including Nagaland with a targeted goal of 24x7x365 power supply; Rs 5,000 crore for 2G mobile coverage; National Sports University in Manipur; setting up of 6 new Agriculture Colleges in North-East to make North-East as India's Capital of Organic Agriculture; etc. will really change the face of the Region if they are implemented as announced. All these were in the Union Budget and, otherwise, no additional economic package for any particular State of the Northeast was announced during his visits.

While attending the two great functions at Imphal and later at Kisama, Kohima, Modi was deeply impressed by rich cultural heritage, amazing bio-diversity and salubrious climate where he made emphasis for the growth and promotion of tourism which would ensure economic boom for the Region. There were different opinions in these areas. Yet, to turn these nature's gifts into major "tourism industries," we need a lot of expertise to overhaul the whole process and systems so that "tourism industries" can come into a reality. The current practices will not economically benefit the States particularly Nagaland and Manipur because it is less than two-week affairs in a year with meager budgets. If Modi really believes that Northeastern Region has the potential for tourism industries for their economic development, then the respective State Governments should be asked to work out as to how sustainable tourism programs can be initiated. These State Governments cannot go for large scale tourism activities unless and until the Center generously provides funds. And once proper tourism infrastructures are there and then the maintenance part in the coming years may not be that expensive.

His assuring to provide 2G mobile facilities in the Region was seen that he was not properly briefed. Because, such facilities were already there in the Region since his predecessor's time.

The people were so hopeful that he would say something "concrete" for the settlement of the Naga political issue because he himself soon after assuming his office announced that solution to the longstanding Naga political issue would be found within eighteen months. So, the people of Nagaland were fully confident that he would bring a "Message" with regard to settlement of the Naga political issue. But he stunned the Nagas as well as other people of the Northeast by not touching on the Naga issue throughout his inaugural speech at the "Hornbill Festival 2014."

The people also thought that he would at least announce an "economic package" for the State of Nagaland like Vajpayee in 2003. But Modi, unlike the past Prime Ministers, did not have any penchant for granting spree of "economic packages" to any Northeastern States.

Strangest things, however, took place in Nagaland prior to his visit to the State that some concerned citizens and intellectuals had openly come out against granting any "financial packages" to the State. Some had even demanded that the Government come to out with proper financial statements of past records before any grants happening. This is one area where Zeliang should seriously ponder over as to why such an unprecedented situation came up. There is something terribly wrong and we have to find a remedy for it.

CHAPTER TWO

MODI MISSED HISTORIC OPPORTUNITY

Naga political issue has been so dearer to the Naga people. They have been living and growing up with the issue. The issue would be always central – be it during election campaigns, conferences of Naga student bodies, conferences of Naga civil societies. It just came in their lives.

The Naga people were overjoyed when the first ever ceasefire was declared between the Government of India and the Federal Government of Nagaland (FGN) on 6 September 1964. This ceasefire was a hard earned one and prominent Indian political leaders, Naga leaders, and even foreigners were thickly involved in the making of this historic and unique ceasefire.

It may be mentioned that Nagaland Baptist Church

37

Council (NBCC) was key in effecting this unique ceasefire between the Government of India and the FGN. They had set up Nagaland Peace Mission with renowned persons like Jayaprakash Narayan, a Sarvodaya leader, Reverend Michael Scott, a British citizen and Bimala Prasad Chaliha, the then Chief Minister of Assam as Members.

The church leaders persuaded the Government of India to halt their military operations for eight days in four villages. During this period, the church leaders along with Rev. Michael Scott visited FGN leaders and discussed the importance of having a ceasefire with the Government of India so as to start political talks for finding a solution to the Naga issue. The FGN leaders verbally conveyed their willingness to have a ceasefire with the Government of India. That was how things were shaped to reach a logical conclusion for entering into a first ever official ceasefire between the Government of India and the FGN on 6 September 1964.

Following the ceasefire, both parties started holding talks within a few months. The primary objective of the ceasefire was to create an atmosphere to find an honorable solution to the Indo-Naga political issue. Talks were held at various places in Nagaland like Chedema, Khensa, etc. And finally it was elevated to the Prime Ministerial level. Prime Minister Indira Gandhi and Naga delegates led by Ato Kilonser (Prime Minister), Gughato Sukhai held talks at New Delhi.

In the 6th round of talks in October 1967, between Mrs. Gandhi and Sukhai, the talks broke down. Later, the Government of India had unilaterally abrogated the ceasefire in August 1972. In spite of breaking down of the historic ceasefire, FGN still observes this "historic Indo-Naga ceasefire" annually on 6 September.

The interesting part was why the Government of India, after a few months of granting Nagaland Statehood, had to declare first ever official ceasefire with the Naga underground group.

On one side, India had to see the nascent State's well-being and security, on the other they had to deal with the Naga underground leaders to see that the first ever ceasefire was maintained and talks followed. After eight years, the Nagaland State survived, while talks with FGN broke down. Violence reared its ugly head again leading to signing of the infamous Shillong Accord of 1975. The Accord, unfortunately, became a bone of contention among the leaders of NNC. Some influential leaders broke away from NNC and formed NSCN in 1980. Again it split into two in 1988—one headed by Isak Chishi Swu and Th Muivah and the other by SS Khaplang and Dally Mongro.

It took 33 years to have another ceasefire with the Government of India. It was on July 25, 1997, Prime Minister IK Gujral announced in Parliament that the Government of India entered into a ceasefire with NSCN (IM). At home, we were all taken aback when the Prime Minister announced the ceasefire with NSCN (IM). The ceasefire declaration paper signed by NSCN (IM) Chairman Isak Chishi Swu was received by only one paper in Nagaland—"The Daily Review, Kohima"—edited by Mheisizokho Zinyu.

Few of us in media did not know what to do thinking whether the ceasefire document was correct. We along with Zinyu rushed to Chief Minister's official residence to meet him and confirm whether the ceasefire was really done. SC Jamir confirmed it and also simultaneously declared from his side about the Suspension of Operation (SoO) against the cadres of NSCN (IM) with immediate effect.

One thing we all should understand is the ceasefire with the Government of India simply didn't happen. In order to reach such a costly affair, so many stakeholders played their parts. You need to build a bridge of understanding through various channels.

NSCN (IM) was arguably the most powerful insurgent group when the Government of India struck a ceasefire with them. And who believed that Swu and Muivah would be coming to Nagaland one day and have free interactions with their people? But it happened. Successive Prime Ministers like Rajiv Gandhi, PV Narasimha Rao, HD Deve Gowda, Atal Bihari Vajpayee and their close confidants had immensely contributed their shares to reach this stage.

While maintaining a ceasefire with NSCN (IM), the Government of India declared another ceasefire with NSCN (K) in 2001. Unfortunately, after a decade, it (NSCN-K) suffered splits. But even after this development, the Center declared that they would continue to maintain ceasefires with both of them.

Therefore, when Prime Minister Modi announced a "timeframe" of resolving the Naga political issue, nobody disbelieved him.

Surprisingly, he is the only Indian Prime Minister who did not touch on the Naga issue during his two-day visit to Nagaland on November 30 and December 1, 2014. His complete silence on the Naga issue in his inaugural address at the "Hornbill Festival 2014" had actually stunned the massive crowd at the venue, sending confused environment wondering what he was up to the Naga political issue.

Was he really serious on the Naga issue or what would be the fate of it at this juncture?

However, many political pundits and media veterans in the region did not buy his "timeframe" idea for settlement of the Naga issue. The Naga issue has today become more compounded unlike the 60s, 70s or even 80s. Today there are many groups which are, in fact, in ceasefires with the Government of India.

His not touching on Naga issue did not make sense in any way because his Government had been in talks with NSCN (IM) while maintaining ceasefires with GPRN/NSCN (NSCN-KK), and NSCN (K) then. He knew very well about the ceasefires with the Naga underground groups. It would have been so meaningful and historic if he said at least his stand on the Naga political issue during his visit to Nagaland. He missed a historic opportunity.

Even many memoranda including the State Government's (Nagaland) and other open letters poured in specifically urging him to expedite the political dialogue for an early resolution to the longstanding Indo-Naga political issue.

It is because of the unresolved Naga political issue, the desired level of the peaceful environment is not prevailing in the Region particularly in Arunachal Pradesh, Assam, Nagaland and Manipur. It is, therefore, crucial to resolving the issue in a time-bound manner and Modi lost one of the golden opportunities to share at least his mind with regard to the settlement of the Naga political issue. He could have asked the Naga people to be prepared to set the ball rolling by opening multiple dialogues amongst them, and most importantly, with sections of people particularly from Arunachal Pradesh, Assam, and Manipur to draw up a comprehensive contributory mechanism so that solution to the longstanding Naga political issue is arrived at soon. He could have asked Chief Ministers of Arunachal Pradesh, Assam, and Manipur to extend supports towards finding a solution to the Naga issue.

Interestingly, Modi failed to join lunch arranged in his honor at the Hornbill Festival venue. Soon after he finished his speech, he was taken to some stalls and later straight taken to the Assam Rifles Helipad, Kohima. He was reported to have his lunch inside his aircraft at the Helipad.

All the past Presidents and Prime Ministers whenever they visited Nagaland enjoyed food and hospitality of the Nagas. Former President Pratibha Patil along with her husband Devisingh Ransingh Shekhawat visited Kisama Heritage Village in 2011. President Pranab Mukherjee graced the historic occasion of the 50th Anniversary of Nagaland Statehood celebration which coincided with the opening of the Hornbill Festival on December 1, 2013, at the Naga Heritage Complex, Kisama.

Modi's dynamism and charisma as the Prime Minister of this great country are, without a doubt, admirable. He is undoubtedly the most powerful Prime Minister with 282 BJP MPs including him in the Lok Sabha, crossing half-mark of the Lower House strength, besides allies in his Government. No wonder, he has been ranked as the world's ninth most powerful person by Forbes Magazine in a 2015 list and in its list, Russian President Vladimir Putin has been ranked as the world's top most powerful person. The famed Magazine (Forbes) while releasing the list of the world's powerful persons of 2015 at the same time said governing 1.2 billion people in India requires more than "shaking hands" and that Modi must pass his party BJP's reform agenda and keep "fractious opposition" under control.

There are many schools of thought coming up after Modi's visits in the Northeastern Region. Several remarks were already made on his meteoric rise as an undisputed national political leader and the Northeastern people, by and large, showered their blessings, praises and happiness on his pragmatism, workaholic style of functioning and pushing the Region to go on war footing developmental mode. The people of the Region believed that his visits to the Northeastern Region might change the course of their dream journeys. He had shown to the people that the Governments, be it the State or the Center, are for the people who are supreme in democracy and nothing else.

CHAPTER THREE

MODI'S FIRST STEP OF APPOINTING AN INTERLOCUTOR FOR NAGA TALKS

The first step of Prime Minister Modi was to appoint a new Interlocutor for the Naga talks. Within three months of assuming his office, Modi could appoint RN Ravi, currently Chairman of the Joint Intelligence Committee (JIC), as new Interlocutor for the Naga peace talks. His action had only shown that he was sincere towards finding a solution to the Naga issue.

However, NSCN (IM) and some Naga civil societies had reacted to Ravi's appointment as new Interlocutor for the resumption of the Center-NSCN (IM) talks. Their objections to Ravi's appointment as Interlocutor was related to the latter's one article – "Nagaland: descent into chaos" - appeared in The Hindu on January 23, 2014. They said Nagaland needs a neutral Interlocutor without any prejudices.

Nagaland Governor Acharya came out appealing the Naga people to give a chance to Ravi and let him start resuming political talks with Naga underground groups. Ravi wrote that particular article before, but he had been appointed by the Modi Government as new Interlocutor for the resumption of political negotiations with Naga underground groups. So now, naturally he had to conduct political talks with the Naga underground people in line with the Modi Government's genuine desire for expediting and resolving the protracted Naga issue, the Governor explained.

Ravi's predecessor, RS Pandey, was appointed as Interlocutor for the resumption of talks with NSCN (IM) in February 2010. Pandey, a 1972 batch Indian Administrative Service (IAS) officer, belongs to Nagaland cadre. He served as Chief Secretary in Nagaland. He resigned as Interlocutor on the eve of the 2014 Lok Sabha elections after announcing that he would be contesting the polls (2014 Lok Sabha elections) from West Champaran, Bihar, in BJP ticket. After his resignation, talks between the Government of India and NSCN (IM) could not be held. For nearly nine months, the Government could not appoint an Interlocutor.

In fact, Pandey could really strike the cord and hammer out many differences. He even came out with the formula of "Shared Sovereignty" to solve the long drawn out Naga political issue. Many including the mainland scholars questioned his idea of "Shared Sovereignty" to resolve the longstanding

Naga political issue. According to him, they nearly settled the issue in 2013.

Ravi's attending the 26th General Conference of Naga Students Federation (NSF) on May 14, 2015, at Khonoma was historic in many ways. First, he was an envoy of the Government of India to Naga political negotiations. Two, his attending the Conference at a birthplace of legendary Naga freedom fighter AZ Phizo was significant. Third, his coming to Nagaland had softened the rigid stand of the Naga people who were initially opposed to his appointment as "Delhi's Interlocutor" for the Naga peace talks.

Ravi is not new to the Naga political history. He retired as Intelligence Bureau (IB) Special Director in 2012 and is Chairman of JIC.

He knows internal security issues and nitty-gritty of northeast insurgencies. As chief of premier intelligence club of the country, his primary job was to brief the Prime Minister of many vital issues, particularly security-related matters of the country.

Even Shyamall Datta, before becoming as the Governor of Nagaland, attended even Center-NSCN (IM) meetings because he was chief of IB. He was busy setting things right for the smooth discussion between the Government of India and NSCN-IM. He was present in a number of talks between leaders of the outfit and representatives of the Government of India held at various parts of the world. Sending him right after his retirement from the IB as the Governor of Nagaland by the then NDA Government under Vajpayee was mainly to help expedite the ongoing peace process and see grounds for strengthening the process and create a peaceful environment. And it was no wrong choosing a high profile man who had vast knowledge on country's issues and problems to become the Governor of Nagaland. It was rare having such a man who had the knowledge of the Naga issue as Governor, although he, as Governor, might have a limited role to play but when he himself knew the subject of the ongoing peace process, it carried sense and those players in the theater could no longer undermine him.

Ravi was, however, critical of Naga insurgents and peace process as could be seen from his past write-up which became the sore point compelling Naga civil societies to initially oppose to his appointment as "Delhi's Interlocutor for the Naga peace talks." Pressures were mounted on the Government to such an extent that the Home Ministry had even forwarded a fresh proposal to replace him, but it was turned down by the PMO. The rest is history.

But seeing his mind on the current Naga peace process after he spoke out at the 26th General Conference of NSF at Khonoma and afterward to media persons, he was only on the expected lines. Nothing new! Nothing extra! The least the people expected from his visit, of course, was that he would endorse Modi's assurance of "timeframe" for settling the Naga political issue in 18 months. This remark of the Prime Minister was even quoted none other than by Nagaland Chief Minister Zeliang.

Although the Nagas were stunned by Modi when he did not utter a single word on Naga issue while delivering his historic inaugural speech at the "Hornbill Festival" on December 1, 2014 at Kisama, and the day also coincided with the "Nagaland Statehood Day Celebration," some simply thought that since he had already assured a "timeframe" for solution to the Naga issue within 18 months, he might not have felt it necessary to mention it again. Even Zeliang was taking that way.

CHAPTER FOUR

MODI'S FORMULA - THEORY FOR NAGA SOLUTION - DEBATE & TWO-DAY DISCUSSION ON NAGA ISSUE IN NAGALAND ASSEMBLY

After Modi's becoming the Prime Minster at the Center, things have been fast moving in different directions. His NDA Government seems to be in a hurry to strike some kind of deal with the NSCN (IM). The lawmakers in Nagaland had been wondering as to what type of fate and outcome of the ongoing political negotiations would be under the supervision of Modi through Interlocutor Ravi.

Individual meetings with the Central leaders on the ongoing Naga peace process were hardly any productive.

The Members of the 11th Nagaland Legislative Assembly formed a Joint Legislators' Forum (JLF).

Actually, it was momentous in the history of Naga political issue when the entire 60 legislators under the banner of JLF could boldly display a show of unprecedented unison in front of Central leaders of Dr. Singh's UPA-II regime for the cause of settlement of the Naga political issue. They also met then Leader of Opposition Sushma Swaraj, who is now Minister for External Affairs, and leaders of various national political parties. They also met leaders of various Naga underground groups, Naga civil societies, and ex-parliamentarians.

But, sadly, they lacked courage to influencing the Government of India and NSCN (IM) to make their "Agenda" public. Today, the Naga peace process is 18 years old, but much to the chagrin, none of the party – be it the Zeliang Government or the Center or the NSCN (IM) – could make the status of the process public.

Regrettably, JLF did not work as desired and it was short-lived due to differences cropped up between the Opposition Congress and the ruling NPF.

The Members of the 12th Nagaland Legislative Assembly came up again with the idea of forming Nagaland Legislators' Forum (NLF) like JLF to collectively urge the Naga underground leaders and representatives of the Government of India to expedite their political talks for an early solution to the longstanding Naga political issue.

So, they finally formed the Nagaland Legislators'

Forum (NLF) on May 25, 2015 with an intended vision to expedite the Naga political dialogue. Assembly Speaker Chotisuh Sazo is the Convener of the Forum. After about 51 days of formation of the Forum, a 19-Member Parliamentary Working Committee (PWC) of Nagaland under the banner of NLF went to Delhi in the middle of July, 2015 and met Modi, Home Minister Rajnath Singh, Union Minister for Home Kiren Rejiju and Ravi.

They informed Modi of the decision taken during their meeting on July 6, 2015 to request Naga Hoho (NH) and Eastern Nagaland Peoples Organization (ENPO) to send a delegation to meet SS Khaplang, Chairman of NSCN (K), to convey the desire and request of the Committee, the State Government and the people of Nagaland for resumption of the ceasefire agreement between the Government of India and them (NSCN-K). They also urged him not to attempt with any kind of piecemeal solution to the longstanding Naga political issue as past piecemeal solutions had only spawned more bloodshed rather than ending the issue.

The Prime Minister was told how the Naga people had been living under fear of the controversial Armed Forces (Special Powers) Act (AFSPA), 1958. The recent extension of the Disturbed Areas Act (DAA) in the entire State of Nagaland for another one year has only brought the memories of sufferings the Naga people had under the shadow of it.

In a gazette notification, the Home Ministry said that it was of the opinion that the whole State of Nagaland is in such a disturbed or dangerous condition that the use of armed forces in aid of civil power is necessary. DAA came into force from June 30, 2015, and this decision came almost a month after NSCN (K) attacked an army convoy in Manipur's Chandel district and killed 18 soldiers.

The PWC Members of Nagaland showed Modi their anguish on the extension of DAA in Nagaland for another one year. This had come at a time when the people of Nagaland expressed their desire for peace. The AFSPA becomes effective in areas declared as "disturbed" and it only vitiates the peaceful atmosphere necessary for a peaceful resolution to the Naga political problem. They have demanded that the Act be lifted for the sake of confidence building amongst the Naga people and to facilitate an early solution of the Naga political problem.

The most interesting part was what the Central leaders including the Prime Minister told them of their minds as to how they would go about in finding a solution to the protracted Naga political issue.

So, when the PWC Members met Modi at his official residence in Delhi, he told them:

"You expect 100%. (But) If I give you 80%, (it) doesn't mean I will not give 20%."

"If I give you a solution and if it is not accepted to

53

you, I am afraid (that) my solution will be more (of a) problem to you."

"Will Naga people accept what I decide? When it happens, it should not go unresolved."

"If peace comes, it must come in toto."

"Every single Naga is important in bringing the solution."

Interestingly, Modi's "80%" formula for the Naga solution sparked intense debate in the Naga areas. It also prominently dominated in the two-day discussion on the Naga political issue on 23 and 24 July 2015 in the 9th Session of the 12th Nagaland Legislative Assembly. The Session started from July 21 and ended on July 27, 2015, and arranged these two days – July 23 and 24, 2015 – for discussion on the Naga political issue.

Strangely enough, nobody knew the exact nature of Modi's "80%" formula for the Nagas solution. Examining his sophisticated words, it is possible that he may not give his 80% formula also.

Was he telling that he was prepared to give 80% to NSCN (IM) for the fact that the Government of India has been engaging in political negotiations with them? When and how and to whom, is he going to give the other "20%?" Is this 20% also to be given to NSCN (IM)? No one knows.

But will this concept of approaching to the Naga

issue be workable or acceptable for the fact that there are other Naga National Groups such as GPRN/NSCN(NSCN-KK), NSCN(R) which are also in truce with the Government of India? NSCN (K), after maintaining truce for 14 long years with Delhi, unilaterally abrogated it in March, 2015. Yet, the Government of Nagaland and many civil societies have been urging the Government of India and the outfit for resumption of their ceasefire agreement.

If you know what is that "80%," then there is every possibility to know what is that remaining "20%" too. But nobody asked Modi so far what was that "80%" he was talking about.

After deciphering Modi's terse remark – "If I give you a solution and if it is not accepted to you, I am afraid (that) my solution will be more (of a) problem to you," it can be safely concluded that he knows very well that any solution for the settlement of the Naga issue is given, and if it is not accepted, it will become a problem to them. It appears that he starts knowing the complexities in the Naga political issue and the peculiarities of the Naga people. He must also be wondering that in spite of many accords and agreements since 1947, the solution to the Naga issue still remains elusive. His predecessors starting from Pundit Jawaharlal Nehru to Dr. Manmohan Singh gave their best to find a settlement to the Naga political issue, yet the issue remains unresolved. That is the reason why he forewarned as saying that "If I give you a solution and if it is not accepted to you, I am afraid (that) my solution will be more (of a) problem to you."

Further his words that - "Will Naga people accept what I decide? When it happens, it should not go unresolved" - only show that he still has doubt on the Nagas. It is only natural for the Nagas to start thinking when he said, "If I give you 80%, (it) doesn't mean I will not give 20%." Some doubt has been cast upon this "80%" as well as "20%". They have to be plainly and succinctly explained for the Nagas to understand.

Modi, however, stated that "If peace comes, it must come in toto." He also explained that "Every single Naga is important in bringing the solution."

But his other remarks – "When it happens, it should not go unresolved?" – sound threatened and imposed.

It is true that no one likes to be belittled how weak and small they are. It doesn't work when you come with roses in one hand and a gun in another hand. Somebody in Nagaland keeps saying he has guts to solve the Naga issue but such "guts" will not solve Naga issue.

We have to learn lessons from GK Pillai, former Union Home Secretary as he could really make unprecedented rapport with the people of the Northeast India. Perhaps, he was one of the best high profile bureaucrats this country had produced so far.

He was instrumental in bringing unprecedented closeness between the people of the Northeast and the Government of India. As Union Home Secretary, he tried his best to extend all possible and positive support to the ongoing peace process between the Government of India and NSCN (IM) and also other groups that were in ceasefires. He could develop a good rapport with almost all the civil society groups from the Northeast. In fact, he got an opportunity to become closer to the people of the Northeast when he was first assigned as Joint Secretary (Home) to look after the affairs of the Northeast. He also used to draw flak from various quarters particularly the political circles for his outspokenness when he was Joint Secretary in-charge of the Northeast in the late 90s. At times, his outspokenness irked the leaders of NSCN (IM). One of the biggest achievements he had as Union Home Secretary is he could win the hearts of the Northeast people. In fact, no any other Indian Home Secretaries in the post-India Independence could become closer to the people of the Northeast as he did.

After becoming the Union Home Secretary, Pillai was closely monitoring the situation in the entire Northeast. He was always concerned for the development of the Northeast and used to visit the remotest areas of the Region. He was perhaps the first high-profile Indian bureaucrat who was widely loved by the people of the Northeast and also the most accessible high-profile official at Delhi, even when he was Union Home Secretary. He knows that the power lies with the people and their voice is supreme.

He enjoyed the confidence of both former Prime Ministers of India - Vajpayee and Dr. Singh.

We remember how Atal Bihari Vajpayee won the hearts of Nagas when he had genuinely shown his love, care and concern for them, and more importantly, while respecting their "unique identity." "Let there be no doubt in anyone's minds that we are as keen as you are to achieve permanent peace with honor and dignity for the people of Nagaland. We fully respect your unique identity. It will be protected. We are proud of your culture. It too will be protected," he said while attending the "First Convocation of Nagaland University" on 28 October 2003 at the Central Secretariat Plaza, Kohima.

What is lacking today in the leadership of the country is their "love, care, and concern" for the people of the Northeast. They also lack their wisdom and diplomacy. The solution is possible only when we understand each other and respect each other's values, cultures, and traditions.

Actually what Modi said to the Members of PWC of Nagaland was "highly sophisticated" which common men will hardly understand? Minister for National Highways Nuklutoshi while taking part in the two-day discussion on Naga political issue in the Nagaland Assembly described as "highly sophisticated" the words and statements of Modi saying that they would not be easily understood by their people. His fear is that unless the Naga people understand the sophisticated system of the Naga talks, things will "simply remain as it is." "It will be highly unworkable if tomorrow the Prime Minister takes a decision on the Naga issue and gives it to us without the consent of our people," he stated. "It will just be another 16-Point Agreement."

"We have to simplify the sophisticated system of the Naga talks and with that, we have to go back to the people with the slogan 'Unity for Solution' and go according to our cultures and traditional systems. We have to take decision from there," the Minister pointed out and further elaborated that even the Village Council could not take a decision if a clan objected. "These traditional systems and cultures still strongly prevail in the Naga villages," he reminded.

The Naga legislators must go back to their people and start working from their respective village levels to tribal body levels to district levels and take resolutions and culminate at Kohima for a final resolution to be submitted to the Government of India. "The Government of India is asking us to come with a formula for the solution to our Naga issue, whereas we are still demanding a solution from them," Nuklutoshi said.

Two days of discussion on the Naga political issue

in the Assembly with almost all the legislators taking part showed very clearly that not a single legislator in the Assembly was aware of the "Charter of Demands" on which the Government of India and NSCN (IM) leaders had been negotiating for more than a decade. It can now be safely concluded that the House was kept in the dark of the political negotiations. They, however, noted that the peace process between the two parties was quite long, and for which, they should urge them to expedite the process for an early settlement to the Naga political issue. After the two-day discussion on the Naga issue in the Nagaland Assembly, the Naga people came to know what Modi and Ravi had in their minds with regard to the settlement of the Naga issue.

The Naga political issue has been always central – be it during Nagaland Assembly Sessions or during general elections or during conferences of Naga civil societies or conferences of student bodies. The Naga people have suffered enough due to this unresolved political conflict. And most of the Members participating in the two-day discussion on the Naga political issue ventilated their strong desires that time had come to see solution to their issue.

Chief Minister Zeliang while initiating the discussion reminded the August House that the DAN Government since its coming to power in 2003 had been giving priority to the Naga political issue even by forming a Political Affairs Committee

(PAC). He informed the House that the Center was already briefed on the latest peace process, besides urging them to lift DAA from the State of Nagaland.

Minister for PHE, Tokheho Yepthomi said a solution to the Naga issue acceptable to all sections of the people might not be achieved at this juncture. Therefore, the Naga people should decide whether to fight for sovereignty or for economic independence at such situation.

BJP Legislature Party leader and Minister for Transport and Civil Aviation, Paiwang Konyak told the House that the State Government was effectively playing the role of a facilitator while the Centre was also making sincere efforts for a solution to the Naga Political Issue.

Home Minister Y Patton said unlike the last Government at the Center, this time the present Government under Modi seemed to be very serious on the Naga issue. So when the Government of India was serious for settlement of the Naga issue, "we also have to be very serious on our part," he informed the House. He stressed the importance of going back to their people, and to educate them of what the Central leaderships had in their opinion towards finding a solution to their issue.

Parliamentary Secretary, Land Resources and Excise, BS Nanglang said aspirations of the young people should also be considered while preparing the roadmap for the solution.

Parliamentary Secretary for Land Revenue, L Khumo said if both the negotiating parties came to a solution, the party would accept it.

While cautioning the Members of the House in talking political agenda, G Kaito Aye, senior NPF legislator and former Minister explained that the developmental process should continue whether the solution to the Naga issue was coming or not as they were there at the cost of their people. At the same time, he urged the Members to fulfill commitments made in their election manifesto and also said that legislators and civil societies should collectively share their views and also reach out to the Naga national workers so as to draw up acceptable formula for solution. He also said, "They have to go back to the people."

Another senior NPF legislator and former Minister, Kuzholuzo (Azo) Nienu cautioned that the legislators' forum on Naga political issue should not become a hurdle in the process of solution. He stressed that the peace talks should be inclusive and they should try to bring all the NPGs together and at the same time all the sixty legislators in Nagaland should be united for finding solution to the Naga issue.

NPF MLA Vikho-o Yhoshu said, "We must remember the aspiration of our people for which the original movement was launched." While speculating that the solution might not be what the original visionaries had hoped for, he, however, urged for more efforts of an inclusive settlement. He cited the tiredness of the people who "feel that any settlement is the solution." Wondering whether leaders were giving enough thought to the likely consequences of a solution not being inclusive, he stressed the need for Naga civil societies and citizens to interact with Indian citizens in other parts of the country and also with fellow Nagas in Myanmar.

Parliamentary Secretary for Fisheries, Shetoyi said all the tribal leaders must be consulted while working for settlement to the Naga issue. He told the House that all the legislators should go back to their respective tribes and initiate unity with other Naga tribes.

NPF legislator, Zhaleo Rio enlightened the House about the genesis of the Naga political issue saying that Naga political movement involved each and every Naga. He disapproved the Center's decision to declare entire Nagaland as "disturbed area" under DAA.

Mhonlhumo Kikon, Parliamentary Secretary, Labor & Employment, Border Affairs, called for a stop to blame games while reviewing Naga history. A broad framework, which takes into consideration the concept of self-determination, was required, he said.

Deo Nukhu, Parliamentary Secretary for Higher and Technical Education, narrated his experiences of atrocities perpetrated by the Indian Army. His village Zhavame was burned down by the Indian Army in 1956. He recalled how the Indian army tortured the men in his village, and moving from one place to another after his village of around 500 households was burnt down by the Indian Army. "The UGs were then treated as the security forces of the people and the Armed forces as terrors of the people," he narrated.

Speaker of the Nagaland Assembly, Chotisuh Sazo, who is also the Convener of NLF highlighted as to how the Naga people struggled during their fight for sovereignty. He also recalled as to how their people were tortured and murdered; besides their houses and granaries were burnt to ashes during the initial period of the Naga struggle. He demanded that DAA & AFSPA should be lifted at the earliest, while urging Naga national workers to reunite in letter and spirit.

Parliamentary Secretary for Eco & Statistics, R Tohanba said, "While aiming for solution, we should also bring unity side by side." Parliamentary Secretary for Agriculture, Benjongliba appealed the Government of India to remove AFSPA from Nagaland immediately and requested the NPGs to make the "Charter of Demands" known to the public.

Toyang Chang, Parliamentary Secretary for New

and Renewable Energy (NRE), asserted that every section of Naga society should be taken into confidence while suggesting setting up of a committee comprising of eminent intellectuals to prepare crucial points pertaining to the Naga political solution and distribute the points to various NGOs, Tribal Hohos, Churches, etc. for wide-ranging discussion.

Stressing on Naga unity, Eshak Konyak, Parliamentary Secretary for Art and Culture said, "If we fail to deliver the desire of the people, it will be a mockery to the rest of the world. We need to go back to our people first. Let us go back to the district and gather the opinions of all public. The voice of the people will strengthen the Naga political issue."

While taking part in discussion on the Naga issue, some Members also pointed out that they should not have another 16-Point Agreement. Although 16-Point Agreement was good enough for them, the Nagas did not accept it because it was signed without consulting the Naga underground group. That is why the Naga issue still defies solution and the Agreement fails to solve the problem till date.

"What have we learned from within the span of 86 years of the Naga movement? Where is the defect?" questioned Apok Jamir, Parliamentary Secretary for Tourism. Suggesting that any solution must be realistic, pragmatic and as far as possible acceptable to every section of the Naga society, he said, "We know that our jurisdiction is within the State of Nagaland and our responsibility lies to the people of 16 tribes of Nagaland but that is not all. When we are talking about the Naga political issue, it transcends beyond the state of Nagaland."

He, however, pointed out that the agreements, ceasefires, done in the past were the best ones happened at that point of time though the solution to the Naga issue still remained elusive.

MLA, Imkong L Imchen; Minister for Social Welfare & Parliamentary Affairs, Kiyanilie Peseye; Minister for Health and Family Welfare, P Longon; Minister for Power, Kipili Sangtam; Minister for School Education, Yitachu; Minister for Rural Development, CL John, Minister for Road & Bridges, Y Vikheho Swu; Adviser for Treasuries & Accounts, Dr TM Lotha; Adviser for LMCP and DUDA, Thongwang; Adviser for Urban Development, SI Jamir; Advisor for NBDA, Naiba Konyak; Parliamentary Secretary for Horticulture, DB & GB, Kejong Chang; Parliamentary Secretary for Irrigation & FC, Jacob Zhimomi; Parliamentary Secretary for CAWD, Y.M.Yolow; Parliamentary Secretary for Planning & Coordination, Neiba Kronu; MLA, S.Pangyu Phom; Parliamentary Secretary for Eco & Statistics, R. Tohanba; Parliamentary Secretary for YRS, Khriehu Liezietsu; Parliamentary Secretary for Home Guards & CD, E.E. Pangteang; Parliamentary Secretary for Soil & Water Conservation, Pukhayi; MLA, Merentoshi Jamir; MLA, Namri Nchang;

MLA, Dr. Longrineken; MLA, Torechu; MLA, Dr. Neiphrezo Keditsu; MLA, Er. Kropol Vitsu; MLA, Pohwang Konyak; and MLA, Tovihoto also participated in the discussion on the Naga political issue.

In his concluding remark after the two-day discussion on the Naga political issue, Zeliang said the legislators took significant steps towards unity and inclusiveness on the Naga politics, with the sole objective of facilitating the early resolution to the Naga political issue. "We are willing and ready to play a more pro-active role in the Naga political dialogue, and that role is 'to facilitate the early and peaceful resolution of the Naga political issue," he said and further explained that their role at the moment had to be limited to facilitating the political dialogue to progress and to urge the parties in the Naga political dialogue to expedite the pace of the dialogue, and to bring it to an early resolution.

"Further, it is my sincere appeal that in the days to come, let this concept of unity and inclusiveness be the overriding principle in the Naga society, as well as in the overground or underground politics, so that real unity can be brought about in the Naga family," he said appreciating initiatives taken by Ravi, Interlocutor for the Naga political dialogue.

"I think we have all accepted that the Naga political issue is no more the prerogative of the Naga nationalist groups alone. It does not belong to any particular tribe or individual. Rather, it belongs to

67

the Nagas as a whole. It concerns all of us, because it is about our collective future. Henceforth, while talking about this Naga political issue, let us use the word 'we' instead of 'I'. I believe this will give the right message to our people and across the country. This way, we can move forward together without hurting each other. If we are united and work together for a common goal, God will surely deliver us from this long-struggling movement," Zeliang concluded.

The need for a solution along with unity, and delivering the aspiration of the Naga people were the main highlights of the NLA discussion on the Naga political issue. Almost all the legislators were given the opportunity to express their views.

■ ■ ■ ■ ■ ■ ■ ■ ■ ■ ■ ■ ■ ■ ■ ■ ■ ■ ■

After discussions on the Naga political issue on July 23 and 24, 2015, the 12th Nagaland Legislative Assembly has adopted the following 5-Point Resolution on the Naga political issue on the final day of the 9th Session on July 27, 2015.

1. Reiterated the earlier resolutions of the NLA demanding integration of all contiguous Naga-inhabited areas under one administrative umbrella, and to urge upon the Government of India to fulfill the same.

2. Urge upon the Government of India and the NSCN (K) to resume the ceasefire agreement.

3. Urge upon the Government of India to withdraw the declaration of the whole of Nagaland State as a disturbed area under the Armed Forces Special Powers Act, 1958.

4. Urge upon all Naga nationalist groups and civil societies to unite and work for the early settlement of the Naga political issue.

5. Urge upon the Government of India to expedite the Naga political dialogue and to bring out a formula for an early resolution of the Naga political issue.

■ ■

After carefully listening to the two-day discussions on the Naga political issue, it is very clear that the Prime Minister and the Interlocutor for the Naga political talks actually disclosed their minds towards settlement of the Naga political issue.

When the Prime Minister told the 19-Member PWC from Nagaland that "If I give you 80% of your demand, it doesn't mean I am not giving you remaining 20%," everyone was perhaps caught napping.

CHAPTER FIVE

DELHI'S SIGNING OF "FRAMEWORK AGREEMENT" WITH NSCN (IM)

WELCOMING "FRAMEWORK AGREEMENT"

REACTING TO "FRAMEWORK AGREEMENT"

The Center had not announced the timing and the venue to clinch the "Framework Agreement" with NSCN (IM). But everyone was again caught napping when the Modi Government at the Center announced the signing of the "Framework Agreement" with NSCN (IM) on August 3, 2015, at Delhi. In fact, Naga civil societies have been questioning the dilly-dallying tactics of the

Government of India in finding a solution to the protracted Naga political issue. But it is surprising to see the manner in which Delhi signed the "Framework Agreement" with NSCN (IM) in a secretive manner. It is now popularly known as "August 3 Framework Agreement."

The "August 3 Framework Agreement" was signed in presence of Prime Minister Modi, Home Minister Rajnath Singh, National Security Adviser to Prime Minister, Ajit Kumar Doval and high profile leaders of NSCN (IM).

However, some political pundits and media specialists in the Region particularly in Nagaland and Manipur got wind of the Center's planning to enter into some type of "Agreement" with NSCN (IM) at any moment. It happened.

It would be much significant and laudable had the Center invited the former Prime Ministers, Interlocutors, Chairmen of the Cease Fire Monitoring Group (CFMG) and Cease Fire Supervisory Board (CFSB), leaders of National Political Parties, Chief Ministers of Northeastern States and even important leaders of civil societies to such a historic signing ceremony.

Buoyed by successful clinching of the "Framework Agreement" with NSCN (IM), Modi announced that with this accord, the Government hoped to open the Northeast to development. The India-Myanmar-Thailand trilateral highway has been held hostage to a number of violent incidents.

Actually, Modi could have at least invited Chief Ministers of the Northeast States if he honestly felt that solution to Naga issue was fundamental to building peace and development in the Region because all the major contentious issues were no longer there in their agenda.

■ ■ ■ ■ ■ ■ ■ ■ ■ ■ ■ ■ ■ ■ ■ ■ ■ ■

When the Modi Government could clinch the "August 3 Framework Agreement" with NSCN (IM), we could only remember the previous Prime Ministers, Interlocutors, media personnel, bureaucrats, writers, leaders of various civil societies, politicians, etc. who had played their roles in shaping process to reach its logical conclusion.

The fact is Pandey was appointed as Interlocutor for the Naga talks in 2010 by Dr. Singh during his second stint as Prime Minister and the process immensely progressed during his time.

Pandey could iron out most of hurdles and bring leaders of NSCN (IM) to a very friendly environment necessary for the solution to the Naga issue. A settlement to the Naga issue was nearly reached in 2013 when he was Interlocutor.

When this author met him at his official residence at Delhi on 17 April 2011, he appeared to be so optimistic for the solution to the Naga political issue, though he was cautious in giving any "timeframe" for the settlement. Yet, he gave so many logical remarks when asked of any "timeframe" for the settlement of the Naga political issue.

"Look, it is true that both sides are sincere. We want a solution and we have made progress, but nothing is final till everything is final," Pandey said.

Pressed further to elaborate, he cited an example in Nagamese in a logical manner, "Moikhan kinika peace process te jai ase, moi laga opinion kobo. Itu Dimapur para Kohima jabole aha nisina ase. Moikhan sub gari loikene, bhat khai kene Kohima jabole ready hoise. Kintu rasta te ki hobo na jane, kile mane monsoon season bhi ase. Landslide kono ba kono ba jagah te thaki bo pare. Hoilebi, chhoto moto landslip to safa korikene jai jabo kintu Kaunba dangor landslide para roadblock hoile, bypass banai kene Kohima punchibole try koribo. Kintu kitiya Kohima Punchibo Kobole tan ase to." (I shall share my opinion with you as to what is the position of the progress in this regard. It is like a journey from Dimapur to Kohima. We all are ready to leave from Dimapur. We, however, do not know what would happen on the way to Kohima because it is monsoon season. There may be landslides. But we shall try to reach Kohima by clearing those small roadblocks. If we can't due to heavy roadblocks, we shall try to make bypasses to reach Kohima. Yet it is difficult to say precisely when we shall reach

Kohima.")

In fact, it is a team work that has been shaping the process to reach the final stage. So many leaders - be it politicians or bureaucrats or leaders of civil societies or writers – had played their important and positive roles over the years preventing the fragile Naga peace process from collapsing on many occasions. The issue became sometimes so threatening to the ethnic diversities of the Northeast people who have been, otherwise, living so peacefully since time immemorial. This unprecedented threat to the ethnic diversities of the Northeast has actually forced the people of the Northeast particularly the intellectuals, academics, writers and leaders of civil societies to go for deeper analysis of the process. It is not an easy task convincing the leadership of NSCN (IM) to come down from their earlier stand to certain level. These leaders should be credited for it.

Former Prime Ministers - PV Narasimha Rao, IK Gujral, HD Deve Gowda, Atal Bihari Vajpayee and Dr Manmohan Singh – had immensely played their parts along with many Interlocutors, Chairmen of CFMG and CFSB, bureaucrats and many influential leaders of civil societies of the Northeast since the signing of the historic ceasefire agreement with NSCN (IM) on July 25, 1997.

Rao declared the Naga issue was "political" and it should be solved politically. He had also secret meeting with NSCN (IM) collective leadership Swu and Muivah on June 12, 1995 in Paris. According to V Balachandran, former Special Secretary, Cabinet Secretariat, the former Indian Prime Minister's (Rao) meeting with NSCN (IM) top leaders in Paris in 1995 was far more important for "India's strategic security than the well-published meeting between Prime Minister Narendra Modi and Muivah on August 3 (2015)."

In one of his writings appeared in The Indian Express soon after the "August 3 Framework Agreement," the former Cabinet Secretary further disclosed that "No one knew about this meeting for two years, when somehow the story was leaked when then PM HD Deve Gowda met Isak and Muivah on February 3, 1997 in Zurich. Later in September 1997, the IM leaders would publicly compliment Rao: 'Among the Prime Ministers of India, he stands out because he alone recognized that the Naga problem could be solved through political means."

Rajesh Pilot also met NSCN (IM) leaders at Bangkok in 1996 and held talks with them.

Gowda also visited Nagaland in 1996 and disclosed about his mind towards the Naga issue.

Gujral made an announcement on the Floor of Parliament on July 25, 1997, about his Government's inking a historic ceasefire agreement with NSCN (IM). At the same time, Chief Minister SC Jamir, while welcoming the accord, announced simultaneously Suspension of Operation (SoP) against the organization (NSCN-IM) with immediate effect.

Vajpayee along with Swaraj Kaushal, Interlocutor, met NSCN (IM) leaders in Paris in 1998 and held very fruitful dialogue.

For the record, he again met them for the second time in Osaka in December 2001and held talks. In this meeting, K Padmanabhaiah was the Interlocutor.

Vajpayee even visited Nagaland in October 2003 and made a historic announcement of the "unique history" of the Naga people.

Dr. Singh, while addressing a Congress election rally at Kohima on February 27, 2008, said his Government had been engaged in a purposeful dialogue with disaffected groups to try and bring a "lasting peace to Nagaland." "We have been open and liberal in our approach and are hopeful that we will succeed in our efforts for an honorable solution," he said adding, "We are willing to go the extra mile for this purpose."

Oscar Fernandez, Union Labor Minister in Dr. Singh Government at the Center, was also instrumental in lifting the fragile Naga peace process to a secured place. NSCN (IM)'s demand to elevate the bureaucratic level talks to a political one was fulfilled by Dr. Singh when he appointed Fernandez to head a Ministerial team to engage in

Naga talks. A major shift in the Naga peace process was noticed after Fernandez-led Ministerial team began talks with the leaderships of the outfit.

It may be mentioned that for the first time, Fernandez along with Centre's interlocutor, K Padmanabhaiah, Joint Secretary, Ministry of Home Affairs, Naveen Verma and Additional Director, Intelligence Bureau came to Nagaland and held discussions with 22-Member strong team of NSCN (IM) led by Muivah along with senior Kilonsers (Ministers) and Steering Committee Members at Dimapur Circuit House on July 31, 2007. In this meeting, both sides agreed to extend their ceasefire indefinitely.

Dr. Singh also learned some lessons from mistakes committed by his predecessor Vajpayee.

The most important chapter in all these happenings is Rao's declaration that the "Naga issue is political and it demands political solution."

After almost 80% of all difficult areas of negotiation have been resolved, it will naturally be easier for Prime Minister Modi to carry over. Moreover, his BJP party's landslide victory in the last general elections also gave an impression to the people of this country in general and the people of Northeast including the members of NSCN (IM) in particular that "Modi can do it." But the fact is he could do it because the ground had already been set by his predecessors and other earlier players in the theater of the Naga peace process. He should not underestimate works of past Prime Ministers as far as the Naga issue is concerned because the issue always remains complex.

■ ■ ■ ■ ■ ■ ■ ■ ■ ■ ■ ■ ■ ■ ■ ■ ■

PRIME MINISTER NARENDRA MODI'S THANKING NSCN (IM) LEADERS, CIVIL SOCIETY LEADERS ...

Thanking Chairman of NSCN (IM) Isak Chishi Swu, General Secretary Th Muivah and other Naga leaders for their "wisdom and courage, for their efforts and cooperation, which resulted in this historic agreement," Modi admitted that the Naga political issue lingered for six decades, taking a huge toll on generations of their people.

Modi, Home Minister Singh, National Security Adviser Doval witnessed the "August 3 Framework Agreement."

The Prime Minister expressed his "deepest admiration" for the great Naga people for their extraordinary support to the peace efforts. "I compliment the National Socialist Council of Nagaland for maintaining the ceasefire agreement for nearly two decades, with a sense of honor that defines the great Naga people," he said.

Modi paid respect to ailing NSCN (IM) Chairman, Swu, who was unable to attend the historic signing agreement. Wishing him "speedy recovery," he said, "Just as his contribution to this agreement has been huge, his guidance will remain crucial in the times ahead.

■ ■ ■ ■ ■ ■ ■ ■ ■ ■ ■ ■ ■ ■ ■ ■ ■ ■

PRIME MINISTER MODI'S REMARKS AFTER WITNESSING SIGNING OF "FRAMEWORK AGREEMENT" BETWEEN GOVERNMENT OF INDIA & NSCN (IM) ON AUGUST 3, 2015 AT DELHI ARE GIVEN BELOW

"I sincerely thank Shri Isak Swu, Shri Muivah and other Naga leaders for their wisdom and courage, for their efforts and cooperation, which has resulted in this historic agreement.

I have the deepest admiration for the great Naga people for their extraordinary support to the peace efforts. I compliment the National Socialist Council of Nagaland for maintaining the ceasefire agreement for nearly two decades, with a sense of honor that defines the great Naga people.

My relationship with the North East has been deep.

79

I have travelled to Nagaland on many occasions. I have been deeply impressed by the rich and diverse culture and the unique way of life of the Naga people. It makes not only our nation, but also the world a more beautiful place.

The Naga courage and commitment are legendary. Equally, they represent the highest levels of humanism. Their system of village administration and grass-root democracy should be an inspiration for the rest of the country.

The respect for the infirm and elders, the status of women in society, sensitivity to Mother Nature, and the emphasis on social equality is a natural way of Naga life. These are values that should constitute the foundation of the society that we all seek.

Unfortunately, the Naga problem has taken so long to resolve because we did not understand each other. It is a legacy of the British Rule. The colonial rulers had, by design, kept the Nagas isolated and insulated. They propagated terrible myths about Nagas in the rest of the country. They deliberately suppressed the reality that the Nagas were an extremely evolved society. They also spread negative ideas about the rest of India amongst Naga people. This was part of the well-known policy of divide and rule of the colonial rulers.

It is one of the tragedies of Independent India that we have lived with this legacy. There were not many like Mahatma Gandhi, who loved the Naga people and was sensitive to their sentiments. We have continued to look at each other through the prism of false perceptions and old prejudices.

The result was that connectivity between Nagaland and the rest of India remained weak across this divide. Economic development and progress in Nagaland remained modest; and, durable peace was elusive.

Since becoming Prime Minister last year, peace, security and economic transformation of North East has been amongst my highest priorities. It is also at the heart of my foreign policy, especially the 'Act East' Policy.

I have been deeply concerned about resolving the Naga issue. Soon after entering office, I appointed an interlocutor for talks with the Naga leaders, who not only understood the Naga people as also their aspirations and expectations, but has great affection and respect for them.

Given the importance of this initiative, I asked my office to supervise these talks; and I personally kept in touch with the progress. I want to especially thank my senior colleague, Home Minister Shri Rajnath Singhji, whose support and advice was invaluable in bringing us here today.

Today's agreement is a shining example of what we can achieve when we deal with each other in a spirit of equality and respect, trust and confidence; when we seek to understand concerns and try to address aspirations; when we leave the path of dispute and take the high road of dialogue. It is a lesson and an inspiration in our troubled world.

Today, we mark not merely the end of a problem, but the beginning of a new future. We will not only try to heal wounds and resolve problems, but also be your partner as you restore your pride and prestige.

Today, to the leaders and the people of Nagaland, I say this: You will not only build a bright future for Nagaland, but your talents, traditions and efforts will also contribute to making the nation stronger, more secure, more inclusive and more prosperous. You are also the guardians of our eastern frontiers and our gateway to the world beyond.

Equally, the rest of the nation will join you in shaping a future of dignity, opportunity and prosperity for the Naga people.

Today, as you begin a new glorious chapter with a sense of pride, self-confidence and self-respect, I join the nation in saluting you and conveying our good wishes to the Naga people.

Thank you.

■ ■ ■ ■ ■ ■ ■ ■ ■ ■ ■ ■ ■ ■ ■ ■ ■

NSCN (IM) GENERAL SECRETARY TH MUIVAH'S REMARKS AFTER SIGNING THE "FRAMEWORK AGREEMENT" WITH THE GOVERNMENT OF INDIA ON AUGUST 3, 2015 AT DELHI:

After the signing of the historic "August 3 Framework Agreement," Muivah assured Modi that Nagas could be "trustworthy" and taken into confidence for any "policy in the Northeast and beyond the frontiers." He further assured that Nagas could still come closer if their rights were respected.

Describing as "visionary" the leadership of Modi, the NSCN (IM) General Secretary said under his leadership, they had come closer to understand each other and work out a new relationship between the two parties on the basis of their uniqueness.

"We appreciate your wisdom, your leadership and your vision to build an enduring relationship between the Nagas and Indians," he said adding, "The Nagas will ever remember you for your statesmanship and your profound understanding of the Nagas with a warm heart for them."

Lauding the courage of Modi on his admitting that the Naga problem was "political issue" and should be solved through "political negotiation," Muivah, however, also admitted that the challenges would henceforth be "great" and also the "responsibilities

83

and the obligations to meet the needs of the people shall be paramount" for both the parties to make the historic endeavor more meaningful.

Recalling former Prime Minister Vajpayee for his concern about solution to the Naga issue, the NSCN (IM) leader disclosed that Nagas were very happy when the Government of India during his Prime Ministership declared the recognition of the "unique history and situation of the Nagas."

He also lauded former Prime Minister Rao for his courage to admit that the Naga problem was a political issue and it should be resolved through political negotiations.

The attitude of the Nagas towards India changed considerably when the BJP Government took a realistic step in recognizing the "unique history and situation of the Nagas." It demonstrated the desire for a lasting and honorable political solution of the issue, Muivah said.

Appreciating Modi's leadership and for his statesmanship shown towards finding a possible final political solution, Muivah said, "Better understanding has been arrived at and a Framework Agreement has been concluded basing on the unique history and position of the Nagas and recognizing the universal principle that in a democracy, sovereignty lies with the people."

"We praise the Naga people and the people of India for exercising unprecedented patience in supporting the Indo-Naga peace process. With all faith and confidence, we believe that an honorable peaceful political solution will be worked out before long," the NSCN (IM) General Secretary said while thanking God and in His mighty work for peace.

■■ ■■ ■■ ■■ ■■ ■■ ■■ ■■■

WELCOMING THE "FRAMEWORK AGREEMENT"

Former Prime Minister HD Deve Dowda and JD (S) leader hailed the Naga Peace Accord expressing confidence that it would usher peace in the region. While talking to reporters at Bengaluru on August 4, 2015, he said, "This Peace Accord with Naga insurgent groups is one of the major decisions to bring peace in the Northeastern States, in general, particularly Nagaland."

"This peace accord with Naga groups is a major achievement to see that there is peace in the region. I hail this decision of the Prime Minister," he said.

It was during his tenure as Prime Minister, Gowda initiated for talks with the NSCN (IM) leaders. He met the leaders of the group during his visit in Switzerland and from this meeting, positive steps were set in motion for coming closer between the Government of India and the group.

After three days of the "Framework Agreement," Rijiju visited Imphal and told the press people that the sentiments of the people of the Northeast States neighboring to Nagaland would not be bypassed while implementing the peace accord between the Center and NSCN (IM). The Center would also see to the sentiments of the people of Nagaland in implementing the accord as it had high regards for the uniqueness of their culture, he said.

Governor of Odisha and former Nagaland Chief Minister, Dr. SC Jamir said the present Peace Accord's major achievement, by and large, was the "exclusion of the two contentious issues: sovereignty and integration."

"This indicates that at long last political realism finally dawned in the scheme of things of the NSCN (IM); the collective leadership of NSCN(IM) should now come up with new ideas to match with the Government of India's peace initiative," he said. "This is a progressive development and exhibits political pragmatism on the part of NSCN (IM)."

"As peace eluded the Nagas for so many years – practically for more than seven decades since India's Independence in 1947; any move towards lasting peace is perceived with optimism," Dr. Jamir said.

Stating that "August 3 Framework Agreement" had stirred the political consciousness of the people of Nagaland, he said the NSCN (IM)'s coming down from its avowed position of holding talks in a third country was not only an indication of making certain concessions but also showing their "political pragmatism."

The people had now come out openly and started commenting, analyzing and weighing different dimensions of the Accord without any reservation which, he said, was a good sign.

Stating that now was time to move forward, Dr. Jamir said, "When other States in the Indian Union have been marching ahead, there is no reason why Nagaland and her people will continue to suffer."

"A bold and forward-looking Government of India is pushing for peace in the region so that its Act East Policy will metamorphose into a vibrant reality. For that to happen, peace in Nagaland holds the key. The sooner it is understood by the Nagas in general and the underground in particular, the better it is for the State and the nation," he said.

A signatory of the 16-Point Agreement, Dr. Jamir said now was the time for the Nagas to "grab the opportunity with both hands and the "younger generation of the Nagas needs to match their counterparts elsewhere in the country."

"Let all the Nagas unite and bury the past, and aim for one final move that settles the Naga issue for once and ever," he said. "But then, the people should know what solution/settlement awaits them in the contents of the Peace Accord of August 3,

2015."

"However, the crux of the matter is that it is like talking about the fish without actually seeing the river. Those coming out in the open only do so knowing only the preamble of the Accord, because the real contents of it still continue to be under the sleeves. Without the full text, it is difficult or may be, unfair to make any comment one way or the other. We would venture to bring home to the readers, the political realities of any Accord whatsoever - be it an Agreement towards political settlement or a Peace Accord," Dr Jamir explained.

Dr. Jamir, however, lamented that the people of Nagaland for whom the Peace Accord had been worked out were in complete darkness as to the exact content of the Accord.

"It is a bitter reality that one full generation of the Nagas has sacrificed everything to see a day when the next generation would live in peace," he said. "So when the real content of the Peace Accord will be worked out, it should take all stakeholders on board namely the people of Nagaland, all major factions of the underground and of course, the State Government."

Nagaland Chief Minister Zeliang, while welcoming the signing of the Accord, expressed confidence that "both the parties have taken into account the aspirations of the Nagas as expressed by Naga civil societies during their interactions with the interlocutor, R.N. Ravi."

"Our people have been struggling for more than six decades for a settlement to the Naga issue and the signing of the Peace Accord is a welcome step towards such a settlement."

While addressing the NPF CEC Meet on August 4, 2015, at Kohima, Zeliang said the declaration of Naga Peace Accord signed on August 3, 2015, was "welcome news." He said it would definitely a result of their "collective efforts and pressures by all concerned during the last 17 years of Naga political dialogue."

He admitted that he was yet to see the contents of the "Framework Agreement" of the Government of India and NSCN (IM), but appealed all not to have a "negative thinking either on the Prime Minister and the Government of India or on the leadership of the NSCN (IM)."

"For me, I firmly believe that Narendra Modi, the Prime Minister has a healthy attitude and respect towards the Nagas, and he will never do what is bad for the Nagas. Rather, we should congratulate the Prime Minister for taking such a bold and positive decision in the style of a true statesman," he said.

Member of Parliament and former Nagaland Chief Minister, Neiphiu Rio, while welcoming the Peace Accord, congratulated the Government of India, the Prime Minister and the NSCN (IM) for signing the Accord.

"It is indeed a landmark occasion for the country, especially for the Naga people who have struggled for more than six decades in our search for permanent peace," he said adding that Peace Accord needed to be welcomed by all sections of people and peace-loving citizens. He was confident that the Accord would bring genuine and lasting peace while strengthening the democratic foundations of the country, also believing that such development would give an opportunity to all sections of the Naga people to come together and unite for the cause of peace and in the greater interest of the Naga people.

President of the ruling Naga People's Front (NPF) Dr. Shurhozelie Liezietsu said when the Peace Accord was signed on August 3, 2015, in New Delhi by the representatives of the Government of India and NSCN(IM), it was taken as the beginning of the process for a settlement.

"They called it 'singing of the preamble.' If that is truly the beginning, can anybody tell the conclusion of the matter at this stage? We trust that there is no hidden agenda and I stand for correction if there is any," Liezietsu said in a statement issued on August 10, 2015.

The veteran regionalist said it was premature to say about a thing which was yet to come, something which could not be fathomed what it would turn out to be. The Naga people on simply hearing the signing of the "Peace Accord," many had become critical, some had become emotional and some had become scared without knowing what was going to happen, some had taken it as a bad dream while many others talked about their imaginations. "Do we project the Naga character in this manner to the outside world," he asked and further explained that those who had real concern for the future of the Naga people, this was the time to have serious consultations with one another calmly and quietly.

"Positive attitude can do a lot at this juncture to create better understanding among the people. Nagas are now passing through a very sensitive and crucial period of time in which our future depends on how we play our role today," he explained. "We believe that whoever is doing the round for a political settlement, they must have been doing their best to protect the best interest of the people to the extent possible while hammering out the points for solution because we are fully convinced that piecemeal solution is not possible and any proposal for solution which is not acceptable to the majority of the Naga people cannot be imposed too."

Liezietsu said it was time to do away with theoretical arguments and to stand on ground realities and contribute if there was something to offer. "The rest of the talking points depend on the progress of the talk including opposition to the Accord by Congress President, Mrs. Sonia Gandhi and Chief Ministers of the three neighboring States," he added.

In his speech on the occasion of 69th Naga Independence Day, General (Retd) Khole Konyak, President, GPRN/NSCN (NSCN-KK), while expressing happiness on the signing of the accord between the Government of India and NSCN (IM), said, "Any solution that may arrive for our brothers in Manipur or NSCN (IM) will be gracefully supported and acknowledged by the GPRN/NSCN. In return, I would also wish that they understand the minds of Nagas living in Nagaland in their process to redesign their future."

"Nagas are brothers no matter how distanced or how big a wall exists between us," the GPRN/NSCN (NSCN-KK) chief said. "At this point of time, we have great concern for our Naga brothers living outside Nagaland. Yet, this can never mean that we forget our dreams while paving ways for our neighbors to realize their dreams."

In his message on the occasion of the 8th Anniversary of "Naga Unification" at their designated camp at Khehoi, around 25 kms from Dimapur on 22 November 2015, Konyak again said, "What pleases the Naga people in Manipur will not necessarily be acceptable to the people of Nagaland. With the Government of India ruling out merger of Naga-inhabited lands into Nagaland, all Nagas must, therefore, live and progress in their own States and domiciles till such time "future generation attains physical integration of Naga areas through historical right and greater political will."

In his address on the occasion of the 8th Anniversary of "Naga Unification," Kitovi Zhimomi, Ato Kilonser of the GPRN/NSCN (NSCN-KK), said that with Muivah admitting that sovereignty and integration was not possible, the Nagas of Nagaland should have separate agenda. He further pointed that Muivah choosing not to make public the contents of the August 3 Accord only "shows that it is not significant to the Nagas of Nagaland."

Zhimomi said if the "August 3 Agreement" was good for the Nagas of Manipur, then they had no issue with it. But for the Nagas of Nagaland, especially the younger generation, there was a need for a separate plan for their well-being as they had nothing to do with the said agreement, he stated.

The Naga Hoho, an apex body of the Nagas, while welcoming the Accord as the foundation towards bringing a lasting solution to the protracted Indo-Naga political problem, fervently appealed the Government of India and the NSCN (IM) to share the contents of the agreement without delay.

In its executive meeting held on August 6, 2015, at Kohima, the Hoho discussed at length in regards to the signing of the "Framework Agreement" between the Government of India and NSCN (IM).

While appreciating the historic agreement signed on the basis of political and historical rights of the Nagas, the Hoho expressed its hope and prayer that any settlement should be honorable and acceptable to the Nagas.

Observing that the people at large were apprehensive and impatient, they appealed each and every Naga not to be swayed away by the rumors through Social Media but to be persistent in the best interest of the Naga people as a whole.

The United Naga Council (UNC), an apex body of Nagas of Manipur, welcomed the signing of the "Framework Agreement" hoping that it would usher peace, development and progress in the Region. While talking to TOI on August 4, 2015, UNC President Gaidon Kamei, while admitting that they were yet to see the contents of the Accord, said, "Today is a historic day for the Nagas as the 6-decade-old Naga struggle and 18 years of political dialogue with the Center (Government of India) have come to a solution. A new dawn for the Nagas has come."

The Nagaland Tribes Council (NTC) said the question of welcoming or rejecting the Peace Accord did not arise when not an iota of the contents of it was known to the public of Nagaland. "The acceptance or rejection of the agreement will solely depend on the merits and demerits of the contents of the agreement," said Lendinokdang Ao and Nribemo Ngullie, President and General Secretary of NTC respectively in a statement issued on August 12, 2015.

They, however, appreciated the bold and decisive

decision of Modi for the Accord attempting to bring a political solution. They urged him to initiate similar approaches to all major NPGs and sign Accords with them to bring an honorable and permanent settlement to the Naga political issue with all stakeholders taken on board.

The Naga Students' Federation (NSF), an apex student body of the Nagas, while admitting that they were also yet to see the contents of the Accord, appreciated the "Framework Agreement." In a statement issued on August 4, 2015 at Kohima, it said, "The Naga Students' Federation is yet to know the contents of the Peace Accord but the framework is truly appreciated. The Federation hopes and believes that the contents of the accord will be honorable, acceptable and beneficial to all the Nagas cutting across artificial boundaries."

The Nagaland GB Federation (NGBF), while welcoming the Naga Peace Accord signed between the Government of India and the NSCN (IM) based on their "unique history," appealed them to make the contents public.

The NGBF urged that all civil societies inclusive of tribal hohos, mothers, students and churches along with the frontal organizations, GBs and Village Councils be invited to a roundtable discussion to settle amicably before a final settlement to solution was arrived at, so that "we the Nagas of all contiguous areas live together under one administrative umbrella for all generations to come." They appealed all groups of Naga national workers to come together to settle together for "one vision and one hope for one nation."

The NSCN(R) on August 6, 2015, welcomed the "Framework Agreement" signed between the Government of India and NSCN (IM) and said, "We highly appreciated the statesmanship shown by the Prime Minister of India, Narendra Modi, in getting the Peace Accord signed on 3rd August 2015. This clearly reflects his sincerity and seriousness in solving the long pending Naga issue."

Lauding Modi for his deep understanding the unique history and situation of the Nagas, the outfit also said the collective leadership of NSCN (IM) deserved to be appreciated for their patience and endurance while looking for the interest of the Naga people. They also appreciated the relentless effort of Ravi in trying to bring an amicable solution to the protracted Naga political issue.

■ ■ ■ ■ ■ ■ ■ ■ ■ ■ ■ ■ ■ ■ ■ ■ ■ ■

REACTIONS TO THE "FRAMEWORK AGREEMENT"

However, the signing of the Peace Accord has not gown down well with other political parties including main Opposition Indian National Congress (INC). Soon after the "August 3 Framework Agreement" was clinched between the Government India and the NSCN (IM), Congress President Sonia Gandhi came down heavily on Modi saying he had not consulted the Chief Ministers of the Northeast.

Calling Modi as "arrogant," the Congress President further accused his Government of insulting the people of the Northeast.

"The Accord may be historic, but the Chief Ministers of the States that would be directly affected were not consulted. Doesn't this show the arrogance of the Government," Sonia said while talking to reporters at Delhi.

"This Government keeps on saying that it will take all the Chief Ministers together. But this step shows that the Government is arrogant. It is an insult to the Chief Ministers and the people of the State(s)," Sonia said. "We're actually shocked that PM didn't even think of taking into confidence our CMs. He did not even think of taking into confidence our Manipur CM, Assam CM, (and) Arunachal Pradesh CM who are directly affected."

Arunachal Pradesh, Assam, and Manipur are the Congress-ruled States in the Northeast. They surround Nagaland, which is ruled by Naga People's Front (NPF) led Democratic Alliance of Nagaland (DAN) since 2003.

Chief Ministers of the Congress-ruled States of the NE – Assam, Arunachal Pradesh and Manipur – where Nagas inhabit –demanded to make the contents of the "August 3 Framework Agreement" public.

Soon after the singing of the "Framework Agreement" with NSCN (IM), Prime Minister Modi had spoken to Nagaland Governor Acharya, Chief Minister Zeliang, Dr. Singh, Leader of Opposition in Lok Sabha, Mallikarjun Kharge, Janata Dal (U) leader, Sharad Yadav, Samajwadi Party leader, Mulayam Singh Yadav, CPI (M) leader Sitaram Yechury, BSP leader Kumari Mayawati, NCP leader Sharad Pawar, Tamil Nadu Chief Minister, J Jayalalithaa, West Bengal Chief Minister Mamata Banerjee, DMK leader and former Chief Minister of Tamil Nadu, M Karunanidhi, Janata Dal (Secular) leader, HD Deve Gowda and Congress President, Sonia Gandhi.

Interestingly, Modi did not speak to Chief Ministers of Arunachal Pradesh, Assam and Manipur – whose roles are crucial in resolving the long drawn out Naga political issue.

Reacting to the signing of the "Framework Agreement," Assam Chief Minister Tarun Gogoi said any move that would affect the interests of his State would be opposed "tooth and nail." He even recalled how he was strongly opposed to the previous NDA Government's move to extend the ceasefire in the Naga-inhabited areas beyond

Nagaland.

Expressing his surprise on not disclosing the contents of the agreement, Gogoi said, "The agreement has been reached after prolonged struggle by the Naga group and it will help in restoring peace and prosperity in Nagaland, but it is astonishing why the clauses of the agreement are kept in the dark."

"We appreciate peace in Nagaland and welcome settlement of Naga issues, but will oppose tooth and nail any move that affects the interests of Assam," he said.

The Assam Assembly on August 10, 2015, also resolved to demand the Central Government to make the contents of the Accord public. The House explained that keeping the Naga Peace Accord a secret amounted to disrespecting to the Federal Structure of Indian democracy.

Participating in the discussion on the resolution, Gogoi said the interests of Assam couldn't be affected or compromised due to any such move.

"The Centre must clarify whether the demand for 'greater Nagalim' has been included or excluded from the framework of the peace agreement," he stated. "If the demand for greater Nagalim has been rejected and the peace agreement does not affect our State, we have no opposition to it."

Explaining for not consulting the neighboring States

when the Mizo Peace Accord and Assam Accord were signed, he said they were done so because it did not affect the neighboring States.

Manipur Chief Minister O Ibobi Singh, who is always opposed to the idea of Naga integration if they are going to affect State's territory, made it clear that his Government would never compromise on the territorial integrity of Manipur. "We will not agree if the peace accord contains any points that threaten the territorial integrity of Manipur," he said.

Manipur Assembly also adopted a resolution on 31 August 2015 urging the Center to ensure that the recently signed Naga 'Peace Accord' did not compromise with the territorial integrity of the State.

Chief Minister Ibobi Singh moved the resolution which said, "this House while welcoming the fresh initiative of the Government of India to bring peace in the North-eastern Region of the country resolves to urge the Union Government to ensure that the 'Peace Accord' of 3rd August, 2015 signed by the Government of India and NSCN (IM) and any subsequent agreements do not impinge on the territorial integrity of the State of Manipur."

The resolution further appealed the Union Government to ensure that all stakeholders, especially Manipur, were taken into confidence, the peace process be transparent and no fresh discords should be brought while attempting to settle the existing one.

The resolution also said, "The House still further resolves to urge the Union Government to amend Article 3 of the Constitution of India by incorporating that prior consent of the State legislature of the affected State(s) shall be mandatory while forming new States, alteration of areas and boundaries or names of existing State."

Against the backdrop of the "August 3 Framework Agreement," the Naga National Council (NNC) headed by Adino Phizo, once again reminded that the "indisputable right of the Nagas have is that Nagas are not Indians and Nagaland is not Indian territory."

In a statement issued soon after the Center's "Framework Agreement" with NSCN (IM), Phizo asserted that no Nagas should be confused with the Naga national stand saying that "NNC is the guardian of Nagaland."

"The Naga National Council (NNC) is not a political party. It is not a government. It is the ultimate national institution of the Nagas," she said. "As such, every Naga has a responsibility to uphold the Naga National Council."

She highlighted specific chapters of how NNC played since its formation in 1946 with an aim to hold the Naga people together in one platform as there was no central authority prior to this. She mentioned how emerging modern India sent her delegation of the Constituent Assembly of India to Kohima and met NNC members, and made an offer to the Nagas to join the Indian Union. The offer was refused. Later, a 10-year agreement offered by the Indian representative in June 1947, wherein the NNC agreed to with certain modification but India broke off its promise with them. And before Great Britain handed over her power to modern India, the Naga representatives declared Naga Independence on August 14, 1947, a day ahead of modern India's Independence on August 15, 1947.

The statement further mentioned that AZ Phizo, on becoming the President of NNC in 1950, immediately began directing the course of NNC into a political consciousness and brought all regions (tribes) together as a nation. He next took a national referendum, because modern India alleged that only a few educated Nagas were talking about their independence. Consequently, "national plebiscite" was conducted on May 16, 1951, by giving a choice to the people to decide whether to stay independent or join India. The result was 99.9 percent not to join India.

In the light of the above mentioned, the NNC President said the "Indisputable right of the Naga have is that Nagas are not Indian and Nagaland is not Indian Territory. The Nagas have every right to be a nation."

In another statement issued by Information &

Publicity Wing of NNC on August 4, 2015, it termed as "very wrong" the manner in which the Government of India entered into a "Framework Agreement" with NSCN (IM) on August 3, 2015, at Delhi.

"It is unfortunate and unpleasant on the part of the Government of India to cheat and lie to the majority of the Naga national groups and the people who have been left behind and neglected," it said.

Stating that one group could not represent the whole and majority of the Naga national political groups and the people of Nagaland who stood for Naga national unity for political settlement in the interest of all concerned, NNC said the Government of India could not be trusted in serious matters as "they always apply divide and rule policy to destroy the Naga people instead of proper political settlement for permanent peace in the region."

It was wondering at Ravi's repeated remarks that their approach would be inclusive taking all stakeholders and groups on board in finding a permanent solution to the longstanding Naga political issue. They said inclusiveness of talk or dialogue with all Naga national groups and stakeholders as stated by Ravi had gone in vain.

Lt Gen Niki Sumi, Military Supervisor (West) of NSCN (K) said the NSCN (IM)'s Framework Agreement with Delhi "intends exclusively for IM" and that they were under no obligation to "either agree or disagree" with the Accord.

The NSCN (K) had walked away from the ceasefire with the Government of India in March 2015.

In a statement issued on August 6, 2015, Lt Gen Sumi further stated that "If it so pleases IM group to append an accord with the GOI, so be it, the NSCN/GPRN is under no obligation to either agree or disagree. It is solely the prerogative of IM group to arrive at any kind of conclusion which they have been striving for the last 18 years and correspondingly the accord itself intends for IM."

He reiterated that the "Naga struggle for sovereignty is an international political conflict between nations and NSCN/GPRN as ever as humbled yet determined to carry ahead this sacred commission passed onto us at the cost of thousands of precious lives of Naga pioneers."

Thepushuyi S Keyho, NNC Vice President, in an Open Letter to Ravi, warned that the Naga peace accord signed between the Government of India and NSCN (IM) on 3 August 2015 at Delhi was likely to bring further division and distrust not only among the Naga people but also between the Nagas and the Government of India as witnessed from their historical experiences.

"Perhaps peace is the guiding force and logic of this agreement as the name of the agreement itself suggests but the truth of the Indo-Naga conflict is about the sovereignty of the Nagas, a cause for which much lives have been sacrificed and peaceful life compromised and not primarily about peaceful co-existence or development even. Peace as desirable as it can be is only possible as a consequent and product of honorable and acceptable solution and not vice-versa," he said.

"Though indications are given on the part of both the Government of India and the NSCN (IM) to be inclusive in their approach, it is still a matter of serious speculation about the framework of the agreement to safeguard the rights and aspiration of the Nagas as envisioned by the pioneers of the NNC," he added.

■ ■ ■ ■ ■ ■ ■ ■ ■ ■ ■ ■ ■ ■ ■ ■ ■ ■

NSCN (IM) leaders seemed to be struggling to give their reasons for not giving contents of the "August 3 Framework Agreement" saying that it was only a "Framework" for the contents to be included after following talks.

Since the Clauses and Contents of the "August 3 Framework Agreement" are yet to be worked out as stated by the parties concerned, it is difficult to draw clear picture or analyze on the would-be bearing at this juncture. Yet, the leaderships of the two should use their political wisdom while working out for the Clauses which should be suitable and workable as per the political and historical environment of the Region. If the leaderships of the country wisely apply their mind at this most crucial juncture, then some chain of positive development may emerge. It all depends on how they apply their wisdom.

Many scholars and writers of the mainland India had, however, already expressed their views and opinions which were published in many national dailies. Unfortunately, many mainland media persons began their news bombardment soon after the signing of the "August 3 Framework Agreement." Several unfounded points totally unconnected with the Naga issue by wrongly mentioning many historical chapters and names were incorporated in their stories. Before the two parties were yet to spell out the nature of "August 3 Framework Agreement," they gave all sort of speculative stories, and even at times looked like they knew everything of the contents of the accord. The mindset of many mainland media should change. It is only because of the strong media forces in the Region, many things have been saved from being destroyed.

■ ■ ■ ■ ■ ■ ■ ■ ■ ■ ■ ■ ■ ■ ■ ■ ■ ■

Many political pundits have been closely observing the fast developing political environment after Modi tersely conveyed his mind and plan to the 19-

Member PWC of Nagaland for settlement of the Naga issue.

It appeared that he wanted to prove that he is a Prime Minister with a difference for the simple fact that his predecessor Dr Singh kept assuring that the Naga issue would be resolved during his tenure (read Dr. Singh's 2nd tenure as Prime Minister) but he failed. Yet, he was still cautious and doubtful when he precisely told of his formula to solve the Naga issue to the 19-Member PWC of Nagaland at Delhi, and this could be dissected from his words – "If I give you a solution and if it is not accepted to you, I am afraid (that) my solution will be more (of a) problem to you. Will Naga people accept what I decide? When it happens, it should not go unresolved."

That was the reason why he specifically asked the 19-Member PWC of Nagaland as to whether the Naga people would accept what he decided. But he cautioned that when such decision was taken, "it should not go unresolved." This means that when they reach such a phase, the Naga people have to take it whether they like it or not.

Modi, however, stated that "If peace comes, it must come in toto," and also "Every single Naga is important in bringing the solution."

We all know that the talks have been going on only between the "Government of India and NSCN (IM)," to be very precise, and most of legislators or for that matter many political pundits as well as media persons have been referring to that. The Government of India's mind is very clear that once a final stage to ink for settlement of the Naga issue is arrived at, they will perhaps start letting Naga legislators know that the solution will be "inclusive."

Today, the Central leaders and many Naga leaders have questioned NSCN (K) on their "unilateral abrogation" of the "Ceasefire" with the Government of India. But none of them has carefully studied as to why the outfit took the highly dangerous step knowing fully that such move would only lead to unwanted development.

If we think 18 years of Center-NSCN (IM) ceasefire is very long, then NSCN (K)'s 14 years of a ceasefire with the Government of India cannot be a short one. If one dissects the nature of these two ceasefires, it will be only exposing the confusing or rather insensitive nature on the part of the Government of India. We don't know whether Delhi knows the ground realities prevailing here in Nagaland or issues critically involving neighboring States particularly Manipur, Arunachal Pradesh, Assam and even Myanmar. General Secretary of NSCN (IM), Muivah, is from the present State of Manipur while the Chairman of NSCN (K), Khaplang is from neighboring country, Myanmar.

Everyone and various intelligence agencies know that NSCN (IM) and NSCN (K) have been deadly rivals since they split into two from their undivided NSCN in 1988 and hundreds of cadres belonging to both of them lost their precious lives only because of clashes between them. Such deadly internecine feuds continued even after NSCN (K) entered into a ceasefire with the Government of India in 2001. But due to interventions of various civil societies particularly FNR, the specter of factionalism had come down drastically and the chasm among factions reduced.

The fact is NSCN (K) during their long 14-year ceasefire with the Government of India had only suffered beyond repair. They had even suffered split while maintaining ceasefire with the Government of India. Interestingly, and for whatever reason, we don't know, the Government of India wasn't prepared to hold political talks, not even once, with the leadership of NSCN (K) in their long 14-year ceasefire, but continues to hold political talks with NSCN (IM) leaderships in full swing since their ceasefire in 1997. This development had made the leaders of NSCN (K) a mockery, besides humiliating them. Had Delhi taken some minimum initiative to even start informal `Political talks` with the leadership of NSCN (K), things would not have happened as we have seen today? Then, suddenly, everyone including some leaders from Nagaland started questioning why NSCN (K) should enter into a ceasefire with Myanmar while maintaining with India.

■ ■ ■ ■ ■ ■ ■ ■ ■ ■ ■ ■ ■ ■ ■ ■ ■ ■ ■

The Naga issue is not something one can make it as a secret affair. It is a political movement of the Naga people starting from their submission of a Memorandum to the Simon Commission in 1929. Everyone is self-analyzing as to what the Prime Minister is up to following the declaration of the "August 3 Framework Agreement."

Soon after the Naga peace accord was signed, the news started overflowing from the national TV Channels and online publications of almost all the national dailies. The people in the Northeast, by and large, did not react to it. The reason why the Northeast people including Naga civil societies remained mum was they did not know the contents of the "August 3 Framework Agreement," so they preferred to remain quiet at least this time. In fact, there were no crackers or jubilation but cautious optimism was prevalent in Nagaland.

CHAPTER SIX

DAN GOVERNMENT'S "FACILITATOR" ROLE TO NAGA PEACE PROCESS & IT'S TIME TO PLAY MORE THAN "FACILITATOR" ROLE

It was so polarizing when the Democratic Alliance of Nagaland (DAN) came to power in Nagaland after dethroning powerful SC Jamir Congress Government in the State in 2003. The first step of the new NPF-led DAN Government was to declare its policy of "Equi-Closeness" to all NPGs. Another policy they had declared was they would remain as a "Facilitator" to the ongoing Naga peace process. A facilitator is someone who engages in the activity of facilitation. They help a group of people understand their common objectives and assist them to plan how to achieve these objectives; in doing so, the facilitator remains "neutral" meaning he/she does not take a particular position in the discussion.

The Government of India had been holding political negotiations with NSCN (IM) and their ceasefire with NSCN (K) was nearly two years old when DAN came to power on March 6, 2003.

The Opposition Congress, which had been in power for more than a decade before being dethroned by the NPF-led DAN, had been maintaining "Equi-distance" to all NPGs. From the beginning, they were opposed to the DAN Government's policy of "Equi-closeness" to all NPGs. Interestingly, Dr. Hokishe Sema, a BJP legislator and DAN Chairman did not approve the idea of "Equi-Closeness" to all NPGs. Another vocal ruling legislator, Huska Sumi, was also opposed to the idea of "Equi-closeness" policy of their Government. They were also critical of the policy of maintaining a "Facilitator" to the Naga peace process.

Then DAN Chief Minister Rio defended his Government's policy of "Equi-closeness" to all NPGs, and, in fact, he came to power by riding on the campaign to find a final solution to the Naga political issue. "Our open door and brotherly approach to all underground groups, together with our policy of Equi-closeness, have been one of the main factors for this relatively peaceful condition," he said on the three years completion of his DAN Government on March 6, 2006. He asked how they would be able to work to find a solution to their longstanding Naga political issue by remaining distanced from NPGs. Disapproving his points, the main Opposition Congress questioned as to how they as elected representatives under the Constitution of India could be close to them.

In fact, the stands taken by the Ruling and the Opposition with regard to maintaining "Equi-Closeness" and "Equi-Distance" respectively to NPGs are two sides of the same coin. It is just the interpretation. Otherwise, it is all the same.

But the logic is how the Government would remain as a "Facilitator" to the Naga peace process. Because it is going to decide the destiny of the Naga people and one fails to understand as to how an elected popular Government should remain as a "Facilitator" to such a political process. The final outcome from the political talks of the Government of India and NSCN (IM) will have a major impact on the Nagas as a whole.

The question comes here is that if they are not a party to "Talks," then will they have rights to interfere into the process or even asking parties in "Talks" to make their "Charter of Demands" public. The danger is what will they say when the Government of India and NSCN (IM) take a final decision to resolve the Naga political issue. In that case, the State of Nagaland will be only a mere audience to the show.

When the Modi Government declared the "Framework Agreement" with NSCN (IM) on August 3, 2015, the Nagaland Government seemed to be struggling to find ways in the event as their

113

policy is only a "Facilitator." The declared policy of the DAN Government has made them handicapped in many ways as far as the Naga peace process is concerned though they started urging the parties in "August 3 Framework Agreement" to take all NPGs and stakeholders on board while working out to find lasting and permanent solution to the Naga issue.

The previous Jamir Government had always demanded that the State Government should know what had been going on between the Government of India and the NSCN (IM). They even pointed out that negotiating parties should not bypass the duly elected popular Government in the State while settling the Naga political issue.

In fact, the new NDA Government at the Center has come to realize the stand of the NPF-led DAN Government in Nagaland and asked them to play more than the "Facilitator" role. They know that the "comprehensive solution" is needed to find lasting and permanent solution to the protracted and complex Naga political issue.

In fact, GK Pillai, when he was Union Home Secretary in 2011, had expressed the importance of the State Government of Nagaland to play more than their "Facilitator Role." He further explained that the Nagaland Government remained neutral, watching the Government of India and NSCN (IM) talks. "We think they (State Government) can do much more than that," he said. "I think they should (State Government) involve in the process."

Representatives of Naga civil societies, during their consultations with Ravi on August 26 and 27, 2015, urged him to take all Naga underground groups and stakeholders on board while trying to find a lasting and permanent solution to the complex and protracted Naga political issue. Even Zeliang while having a Consultative meeting with him at the Conference Hall of the Nagaland Legislative Assembly had succinctly stated that all NPGs and stakeholders should be taken on board while trying to find a solution to the Naga issue.

Zeliang even came out in a clear term that without their "collective efforts and our strong back-up," the Interlocutor would not be able to produce the expected outcomes. He also said the Naga issue belonged to all and "it is no more the prerogative of the Naga nationalist groups alone."

If these are the demands of the Naga people, has the time not really come for the DAN Government to change their declared policy of maintaining as a "facilitator" to the Naga peace process to somewhat more practical and pragmatic. This is the very reason why Ravi told 19-Member PWC of Nagaland when the latter met the former at Delhi that they should play more than their role as a "Facilitator." Because a facilitator is simply not part of the inclusiveness. He also requested them, "What is possible; tell us, we will work together."

These complexities and dangers were noticed by Delhi as they had seen why the Naga issue still remained unresolved even after 16-Point Agreement of 1960 or why the Shillong Accord of 1975 invited more bloodshed among the Nagas. That is why Ravi wisely informed the 19-Members PWC of Nagaland at Delhi that the State government should play more than a "facilitator," indicating that they should be part of the process because any settlement which is to be arrived at will be for all of them. So any solution "should be comprehensive and not a piecemeal solution" and the process should be with an "inclusive approach keeping in mind the basic Naga ethos, Naga cultures, and Naga traditional systems," he said.

PHOTO GALLERY

PM Narendra Modi in Naga traditional attire at the Opening Ceremony of the "Hornbill Festival" on 1 December 2014 at Kisama. Governor PB Acharya (left) & CM TR Zeliang (3rd right).

Chief Minister TR Zeliang (right standing) at two-day discussion on Naga Political issue on 23 & 24 July 2015 in the Nagaland Assembly. (Nagaland DIPR Photo).

19-Member Parliamentary Working Committee (PWC) of Nagaland led by Convener, Nagaland Legislators' Forum (NLF), Chotisuh Sazo (sitting right), who is also Speaker of Nagaland Legislative Assembly met Prime Minister Narendra Modi on 16 July 2015 at New Delhi.

(**Sitting from L to R**: P Longon, Medical Minister; Ajit Kumar Doval, National Security Adviser; Prime Minister Narendra Modi; TR Zeliang, Nagaland Chief Minister; Chotisuh Sazo, Speaker, Nagaland Legislative Assembly and Convener, Nagaland Legislators' Forum.)

(**Standing from L to R**: Dr TM Lotha, Adviser; MLA CM Chang; Phukayi, Parliamentary Secretary (PS), L Khumo, PS, BS Nanglang, PS; Yitachu, Education Minister; Vikheho Swu, R&B Minister; Er Levi Rengma, PS; Dr N Nicky Kire, Forest Minister; Kipili Sangtam, Power Minister; Y Patton, Home Minister; Nuklutoshi, National Highways Minister; P Paiwang Konyak, Transport, IT & Communication Minister; R Tohanba, PS; Neiba Kronu, PS and C Apok Jamir, PS.)

19-Member Parliamentary Working Committee (PWC) of Nagaland led by Assembly Speaker & Convener of Nagaland Legislators' Forum (NLF), Chotisuh Sazo (sitting 2nd right), met Union Home Minister Rajnath Singh, Interlocutor for Naga talks RN Ravi in July, 2015 at New Delhi.

NSCN (IM) General Secretary Th Muivah (left) and Interlocutor for Naga talks RN Ravi (right) after signing the historic "Framework Agreement" on 3 August 2015 at Prime

Minister Narendra Modi's 7 Race Course Road Residence, New Delhi. Prime Minister Modi and National Security Adviser Ajit Kumar Doval witnessing the signing ceremony.

Prime Minister Narendra Modi speaking at the historic signing ceremony of "Framework Agreement" between the Government of India and NSCN (IM) on 3 August at his 7 Race Course Road Residence, New Delhi. NSCN (IM) General Secretary Muivah (sitting 3rd right), Interlocutor Ravi (sitting 1st right), Union Home Minister Rajnath Singh (sitting 3rd left) seen in the picture.

PM Narendra Modi arriving at Kisama to inaugurate the "Hornbill Festival 2014" on 1 December, 2014 with Nagaland Governor PB Acharya (left) and Chief Minister TR Zeliang (right).

CHAPTER SEVEN

"POST AUGUST 3 FRAMEWORK AGREEMENT" CONSULTATIONS

"I assure you that we will always be sensitive to the needs and concerns of the people of Nagaland, as also of the people of other North-Eastern States. Similarly, the people belonging to each State, and each ethnic group, in the North-East should be sensitive to the needs and concerns of their neighbors. Let us leave behind all the unfortunate things that happened in the past. For too long this fair land has been scarred and seared by violence. It has been bled by the orgy of the killings of human beings by human beings. Each death pains me. Each death diminishes us. My Government has been doing everything possible to stop this bloodshed, so that we can together inaugurate a new era of peace, development and prosperity in Nagaland."

~~~~ *Atal Bihari Vajpayee at the "First Convocation of Nagaland University" on 28 October 2003 at the Central Secretariat Plaza, Kohima.*

Interlocutor Ravi's proposed visit to Nagaland on August 24, 2015 had been abruptly cancelled. His proposed visit to Nagaland was to hold consultations with Nagaland lawmakers, Naga civil society leaders, and student and church leaders to get finer inputs from them for giving final touch to settlement of the protracted Naga political issue.

His abrupt cancellation of Nagaland visit might be due to the NSCN (IM)'s proposed 8th Naga People's Consultative Meeting slated for August 25, 2015 at Niathu Resort, Dimapur. All 60 Members of the Nagaland Legislative Assembly (NLA), leaders of Naga civil societies, leaders of student bodies, mothers and church leaders were invited to this Consultative Meeting.

This Consultative Meeting assumed significance in view of the "August 3 Framework Agreement" between the Government of India and NSCN (IM).

The proposed visit of the Interlocutor to Nagaland was also for the same mission. He would have wide range of consultations with the Nagaland lawmakers, leaders of Naga civil societies, leaders of student bodies, mothers and church leaders.

Ravi arrived in Nagaland on August 26, 2015. By now, he must have learned enough to figure out the minds of the Naga people towards a final settlement of the Naga politic issue. It will definitely become easier for him to talk to the Naga people as he had already seen their minds and thoughts expressed during NSCM (IM)'s Naga People's Consultative Meeting on August 25, 2015.

■ ■ ■ ■ ■ ■ ■ ■ ■ ■ ■ ■ ■ ■ ■ ■ ■ ■

At the "8th Naga People's Consultative Meeting," Muivah gave the background of the "August 3 Framework Agreement" which drew mix reactions from various quarters including several Naga leaders. Most of them, while appreciating the signing of the Naga peace accord, refused to comment on it saying they were yet to see the "contents" of the accord. The Naga people have witnessed the history of mistakes and most of them are not willing to see the similar historical blunders again while trying to resolve the longstanding Naga political issue. Their demand is all NPGs and other stakeholders should be taken on board while searching for lasting and final settlement of the Naga issue. Every one of them was against attempting for any piecemeal solution.

Speaking at the Consultative Meeting, Nagaland MP (Lok Sabha), Neiphiu Rio appreciated Prime Minister Modi and leaderships of NSCN (IM) for singing the historic Naga Peace Accord on 3rd August 2015 at New Delhi. "Modi has exhibited exemplary and decisive leadership in addressing the decades old Indo-Naga political conflict," he said.

Recalling Ravi's statement that the Center would reach out to every section of Naga society to solve the Naga issue, Rio appealed the Northeast MPs to extend their cooperation towards finding a solution to the Naga issue.

The Nagaland MP also felt that NSCN (IM) leaderships should exercise "maximum magnanimity with all groups and different sections of society to foster a spirit of brotherhood and unity among our people."

He thanked Naga civil societies, NGOs, tribal hohos, church and FNR for their roles in bringing different NPGs to meet, discuss and join the process of finding a "common ground" that would enable the Nagas to arrive at a realistic position that is honorable and acceptable to the Nagas."

Remembering the past leaders who had sown the seeds of Naga aspirations, Rio said the Naga people owed their present status and the future aspirations to all the visionary leaders before them, beginning from the "members of the Naga Club who submitted our first memorandum to the Simon Commission in 1929, to the bold, decisive and inspirational leadership of late A.Z. Phizo, and all the great sons and martyrs of our land."

"India has recognized our unique history and is

willing to restore our honor and dignity," the Nagaland MP informed and said, "It is time for the Naga family to move forward and join the national and global community by making positive contributions for peace and progress armed with our rich culture and heritage and the vast potentials of our people and of our land."

Niketu Iralu, noted peace activist, while speaking to the "8th Naga People's Consultative Meeting" on the Indo-Naga talks, said, "History is full of examples that a struggle not examined truthfully becomes impossible to pursue, and it ends up destroying itself and the people for whom it was started in the first place. And no Naga will disagree that this is true also of our 'Overground' political process. Here we must be clear the unexamined thinking and living of all of us has produced this common suicidal destructiveness."

He believed that the "consultation idea was God's roadmap and guidance" to the Nagas through NSCN (IM) to "rectify our wrong ways, and revolutionize our inadequate thinking and living so that our society will rise in unity to achieve what is right and best for all, through radical change in all of us, instead of sinking together blaming one another over who is right or wrong."

Iralu recalled what he said in his participation in the NSCN (IM)'s 1st Naga People's Consultative Meeting held at Niuland in 1998. "At the first consultation in 1998 I said that if the NSCN (IM) starting their negotiation with the Government of India succeeded in getting India to recognize Naga sovereignty as understood by the Naga people, the entire Naga public and all the rival groups would simply say "Thank you" and get on to celebrate the achievement together. But if they discovered that Delhi was not in a position to discuss sovereignty because it was too difficult for India, and IM decided to negotiate for something other than sovereignty, they needed to call the different fragmented groups and tell them the truth about the new situation and thrash out together in complete transparency a common position on the terms for political negotiations with Delhi for a settlement of the Indo-Naga issue."

He stressed the urgency that the NSCN (IM) leaderships begin consulting and taking into consideration the "views of all the other factions even if you don't agree with all their points." Such steps would also be the beginning of real reconciliation as this would be deciding together honestly on the most difficult issue over which "Nagas have killed Nagas and the Indian Army has killed Nagas and all Nagas have paid a very heavy price of suffering," he said and further warned that "Failing to do this, history will always judge and things, as you know better, can go very wrong."

Iralu also said the Naga people's deepest "fear and concern" was what would happen after a settlement, and the "greatest gift the NSCN (IM) and the Government of India can give to the Nagas is to guarantee that no violence or threat of violence will be employed in the implementation of whatever settlement may emerge."

Yet no one knew the details of the agreement and the only hope and desire of the their people was that when "it comes it will take our society and whole region forward so that a stability hitherto unknown will become a reality and growth and development in all dimensions will become possible," he stated.

Iralu quoted Bill Clinton's four points he made on a visit to Wales concerning Conflict Resolution:

1. *Present day problems are mostly the fear of the other.*
2. *The need of the day is to think of a future different from the past.*
3. *No one has the monopoly of the truth.*
4. *To befriend a people, you have to understand not only their dreams and hopes, but also understand their worst nightmares.*

On the occasion of the 8th Anniversary of the "Naga Unification" held on 22 November 2015 at the Khehoi designated camp of GPRN/NSCN (KK), Iralu was again invited to speak there.

The "Naga Unification" was initiated by GPRN/NSCN (NSCN-KK) and it completes 8 years on November 22, 2015. The outfit is in truce with the Government of India, and yet to start political dialogue.

Iralu said, "From our conscience will come imaginative, constructive ideas of statesmanship that will be right for all Nagas. It is said 'Statesmanship is doing today what events will force you to do tomorrow.' This kind of statesmanlike leadership is what we urgently need from the leaders of all groups and factions today." "Anything less will keep us in endless distrust and vengeful bitterness against one another. We all know we cannot achieve anything lasting if mutual distrust will be allowed to continue to paralyze us and keep us selfish and tribe-centered," he asserted.

Stating that they were entering a new year and a new situation where "all Nagas of all tribes, factions and parties must take a united solemn pledge that no faction or tribe will use violence and force to gain their own advantage at the expense of others," Iralu said Nagas would no longer allow the "darkness of hatred and violence that they have endured to return."

"The Government of India engaged in ceasefire and negotiation talks with various groups will be held equally responsible if violence and force will be used to implement any settlement and let the Nagas continue to suffer," he warned.

The peace activist also highlighted that in the struggle to become a people and to grow as a nation was the most "demanding and complicated venture" for any people to start and pursue. In the process, the people involved used to make "all kinds of mistakes" because of the "weaknesses and shortcomings common to all human beings." "We the Nagas too have made serious mistakes," he said. "And let us not forget we are just at the beginning of our story."

They have to learn from their "mistakes by maturely and responsibly acknowledging" where they have gone "wrong," he pointed out and further reminded the gathering that their "crisis today is threatening to overwhelm us because instead of admitting our own mistakes, which will inspire others to do likewise, we are blaming one another and this has paralyzed our struggle and our society." "This short-sighted, suicidal folly is provoking the worst, the meanest out of all Nagas. It has brought us to a dead end," he said.

Stating that the occasion was a crucial moment when they together should discover the common meeting ground where they were all the same before their Creator, he said it was all about "the soul and conscience inside each one of us."

"It is the core essence of our personality and our only dependable guide for restoration of trust and unity that will enable us to survive and succeed today," Iralu said. "Conscience is the truest friend of all of us no matter which faction, tribe or party we may belong to."

■ ■ ■ ■ ■ ■ ■ ■ ■ ■ ■ ■ ■ ■ ■ ■ ■ ■ ■

The 3rd Consultative Meeting for the Nagaland legislators and the Members of NSCN (IM) also held on 26 August 2015 at the Chumukedima Police Complex. It said fifty-six Nagaland legislators including Chief Minister Zeliang attended the six-hour marathon Consultative Meeting with the NSCN (IM) strong team. Zeliang, while addressing the Consultative Meeting, warned against going for a piecemeal solution to the protracted Naga political issue by reminding them of the past piecemeal solutions, which only led to more bloodshed. He, however, felt that after the "August 3 Framework Agreement," the Naga political dialogue had entered into a very crucial phase and was now closer to its final resolution than ever before.

The Naga civil organizations, in the interactive session with Muivah during the Naga People's Consultative Meeting, expressed their affirmation that the "August 3 Framework Agreement" must lead to an acceptable and honorable settlement to the Indo-Naga political issue. A resolution adopted after the Consultative Meeting also appreciated the Government of India and NSCN (IM) for signing the "August 3 Framework Agreement" which should lead to an acceptable and honorable settlement to the "Indo-Naga issue." It also resolved to reiterate and uphold the previous resolutions of the Naga People's Consultative Meetings and to ceaselessly strive towards unity in a "spirit of forgiveness and oneness."

During the Consultative Meeting, Zeliang stressed the importance of taking all Naga nationalist groups on board for a formula to resolve the Naga political issue. He urged Interlocutor and NSCN (IM) to take the lead, and while doing so, they would also need the solid back-up and cooperation from the NLF, leaders of mass based Naga organizations, Churches, and FNR.

"In this world, leadership comes and goes. No one can avoid death. But history will repeat our deeds and achievements after we leave this world. Therefore let us do our best to leave behind a worthwhile legacy, for which the Naga people will remember us with gratitude for what we have done," he said.

Muivah was reported to have explained about the "shared sovereignty" and the "Pan-Naga Hoho" concepts during the Consultative Meeting. According to sources, the Pan-Naga Hoho is to look after the welfare of Naga areas which cannot be included in the Naga integration due to geographical location. It will be a statutory body with certain budgetary provisions to function, disclosed the sources. With regard to "shared sovereignty," both the negotiating parties are to share the competencies by respecting people's wishes on "sharing sovereign power" as defined in the competencies where both sides agreed on a peaceful co-existence.

Ravi is yet to spell out the concept of "shared

sovereignty". He only says, "Sovereignty lies with the people."

. . . .

RAVI'S CONSULTATIVE MEETINGS WITH NAGALAND LAWMAKERS, NAGA CIVIL SOCIETIES, STUDENT BODIES, CHURCHES AND MOTHERS

Soon after his arrival on August 26, 2015 at Kohima, Ravi called on Nagaland Governor Acharya at Raj Bhavan, Kohima.

The Governor informed him of the Nagaland Government's request to the Government of India that talks should also be held with other NPGs with whom it had also entered into ceasefire agreements.

Acharya said it was logical and necessary to incorporate views of other groups in the Framework Agreement. Talks should be inclusive involving all groups. On this, he spoke to Home Minister Rajnath Singh even before the peace agreement was signed with NSCN (IM). He expressed satisfaction that both the Union Home Minister and Interlocutor had been meeting all groups including civil societies, NGOs, mothers' associations and individuals.

The Governor assured that the State Government

with all the sixty Members in the Legislative Assembly would work hard with trust in each other to bring honorable implementation of all the Clauses in the Agreement.

Later, Ravi held a series of consultations with leaders of Naga civil societies at Kohima and explained them the position of the Government of India with regard to signing of the "Framework Agreement" with NSCN (IM) on August 3, 2015 at Delhi. He actually told the 19-Member PWC of Nagaland when the latter met him at Delhi about Delhi's "inclusive approach" towards finding final solution to the protracted Naga political issue "keeping in mind the basic Naga ethos, Naga culture, and Naga traditional systems." In fact, he knew very well why solution to the 68 years old Naga issue defied solution till date and he informed them that they were working out for a "comprehensive solution and not for a piecemeal solution."

Nagaland legislators as well as leaders of Naga civil societies were urging the Interlocutor for "inclusiveness" of all NPGs while trying to find a final solution through their "August 3 Framework Agreement."

While meeting with the delegation of Naga Hoho at de Oriental Hotel, Kohima, the Interlocutor assured that the Government of India would not go for a "piecemeal solution" to the Naga political issue and further made it clear that it would be a "comprehensive solution."

He was reported to have told the delegation of Hoho that the Government of India would not commit the same mistake as it did in the past and that was the reason why their present approach was "inclusive" of all concerned towards finding lasting and permanent solution to the Naga political issue.

Requesting the Naga people for their cooperation towards Center's "inclusive approach" to Naga issue, Ravi had disclosed that he already extended invitations to other NPGs for meeting and discussion. According to him, the formula of a Pan-Naga Hoho that was to look after the welfare of the Naga areas, which could not be included in the Naga integration, was very much in the agenda, even "though finer details are yet to be worked out."

In his concept of sovereignty, the Interlocutor said "sovereignty lies with the people" as "no country is independent but interdependent." On this basis of sharing the sovereign power, the Indians and the Nagas would coexist.

It was, however, learnt that the Hoho delegation told the Interlocutor that "Integration is non-negotiable."

The interlocutor also held consultations with delegations of Naga Students' Federation (NSF), Eastern Nagaland Peoples' Organization (ENPO), Eastern Nagaland Women Organization (ENWO), Eastern Naga Students' Federation

136

(ENSF), Naga Mothers' Association (NMA), Forum for Naga Reconciliation (FNR), and the Nagaland Baptist Church Council (NBCC). He explained them salient features of the "August 3 Framework Agreement."

Many leaders, while welcoming the "August 3 Framework Agreement" had cautioned him that the Government of India's attempt to find lasting and final settlement of the longstanding Naga political issue would face problem if all NPGs were not involved in the process.

The ENPO team reminded him of issues facing the people of their areas, and their demand for a separate Statehood.

The ENWO team appealed the Government of India to make all out efforts to bring NSCN (K) back to the ceasefire fold. "The Government of India should play the role of a good father and bring back the estranged child into his fold," they told the Interlocutor and further voicing their concern on the excesses committed by the Indian security forces. They wanted that the Government of India must ensure that the security forces exercise utmost restraint while discharging their duties in all the length and breadth of Nagaland.

The NMA told Ravi that there must be involvement of women in the framing of any solution concerning the Nagas. NMA president Abei-u Meru explained that "inclusiveness" should cover the mothers, irrespective of any NPGs.

FNR told Ravi to take all NPGs on board while trying to find lasting and permanent solution to the Naga issue.

The NBCC leaders, however, stated that they did not meet him to endorse the "August 3 Framework Agreement" but went to listen to him. They told him that the Church stood for "reconciliation, truth, unity and peace."

He also held consultation with Nagaland Gaon Burahs Federation (NGBF).

....

Interlocutor held Consultative Meeting with the Members of NLF on the Naga Political Issue on August 27, 2015, at the Conference Hall of the Nagaland Legislative Assembly, Kohima.

Welcoming Ravi at the Consultative Meeting between the NLF and him (Ravi) at Kohima, Chief Minister Zeliang lauded him saying that he had proved himself to be better than the past Interlocutors. "After having quick consultations with the Naga civil society organizations, and having a feeling of the pulse of the Naga people, he lost no time in producing the first result in the form of the Framework Agreement, which was signed on the 3rd August, 2015 by the parties to the dialogue," said the Chief Minister calling all Members of NLF present to appreciate "his style and approach to the Naga political issue, although we have yet miles to go before we can relax."

"Let us also put our wholehearted confidence and support to the Interlocutor, so that he may be able to take forward the Framework Agreement to its final and logical conclusion," Zeliang said and informing the gathering that one of the greatest assets the Interlocutor had was his "proximity to the Prime Minister, Narendra Modi, whose confidence he is enjoying."

"He should now approach the other Naga nationalist groups, and bring them on board the Naga political dialogue. We are all of the view that the Naga political dialogue should be made inclusive now, if it is really to result in permanent peace to our land," the Chief Minister said. He, however, explained that without their "collective efforts, and our strong back-up," the Interlocutor would not be able to produce the expected outcomes.

Zeliang also reminded Ravi that some of the provisions of the 16-Point Agreement of 1960 made between the Government of India and the Naga Peoples' Convention (NPC) were yet to be fulfilled. "As per the 16- Point Agreement, Article 371A of the Constitution was inserted," he informed him.

"However, the provisions regarding Acts of Parliament not to apply in the case of 'land and its resources' have not been honored in letter and spirit by the Government of India," he said. "The Govt. of India is trying to create problems in the implementation of the Nagaland Petroleum Rules & Regulations duly passed by the Nagaland Legislative Assembly. Similarly, the provisions regarding restoration of transferred Naga reserve forests to Nagaland have not been followed up by the Central Government."

Zeliang, however, hoped that the Consultative Meeting would provide the needed thrust and impetus to take forward the Naga political dialogue from the stage of "Framework Agreement" to the next stage of a detailed, inclusive and conclusive agreement that would usher in a period of peace and prosperity in their land.

■ ■ ■ ■ ■ ■ ■ ■ ■ ■ ■ ■ ■ ■ ■ ■ ■ ■ ■ ■

RAVI EXPANDED CONSULTATION NETWORKS BEYOND NAGALAND TO MANIPUR

V Narayanswamy, Congress' General Secretary and in-charge North Eastern States, however, said that Ravi's visit to Nagaland for consultations with civil societies, State legislators and other stakeholders should have been done before signing the Naga accord and, not making bizarre attempts now. The Congress leader in-charge of Northeastern States said that the process of completely settling down the Naga issue couldn't be reached until the States of Manipur, Arunachal Pradesh and Assam are made part of the agreement.

However, Ravi did not waste time in expanding his consultation networks beyond Nagaland shore. After his consultations with Naga civil societies, Nagaland lawmakers, student bodies, mothers and church leaders, he visited Manipur and held a series of consultations with leading Valley and Hills civil societies at Imphal. For record, he had already visited Imphal twice for wider consultations with the Valley and Hill civil societies and also the officials of the Government of Manipur on the "August 3 Framework Agreement." He explained to them the salient features of the "August 3 Framework Agreement."

Members of the Citizens Committee Manipur (CCM) informed Ravi during his second consultations at Imphal that he should not bring any agreement and development based on ethnic line as the "State is inhabited by 40 different ethnic communities."

Addressing massive gathering at the civic reception held in his honor on 12 August 2015 at Dimapur Airport, Muivah also said that the Nagas were ready to understand with neighboring States and other communities and not confront them as "we will be neighbors forever."

When GK Pillai was Union Home Secretary, he was once asked as to whether the Center would take into account the States of the Region where the Nagas inhabit before entering into a final settlement of the Naga issue. His straight reply was that these States would be consulted before entering into any final settlement of the Naga issue. "Everybody wants solution not only in Nagaland," he said stressing that the "basic aim is that they have to strike a harmony and bring honorable settlement to the issue."

During Dr. Singh's Prime Ministership, he gave green signals to his Home Ministers - Susil Kumar Shinde, and later P Chidambaram – to have parleys with the Chief Ministers of Northeastern States particularly Arunachal Pradesh, Assam, and Manipur. They started engaging in series of consultations with the Chief Ministers of Assam and Manipur to find an amicable settlement of the Naga political issue. Following these developments, Home Minister Chidambaram and also high profile officials from the Ministry of Home Affairs made a series of visits to Manipur and it's Ukhrul District HQs. Muivah hails from Ukhrul District.

Seeing at all these development, things have been going in right direction and, of course, process nearly collapsed on certain stages due to dirty politicization by few narrow-minded and selfish politicians. It was unprecedentedly bent but luckily, not broken. The general publics have today realized that such dirty politicization into the peace process has itself poisoned into the minds of the general publics.

Although it was right step on the part of the Government of India holding parleys with the Chief Ministers of Arunachal Pradesh, Assam and Manipur for finding amicable solution to the Naga issue, the most important thing is they should invite the leaders of important and leading civil societies of these States and start discussing with them. Because, the Chief Ministers of these States alone cannot give their verdicts to the Government of India if the civil societies are also not fully convinced. At the same time, the Chief Ministers of these States should also immediately hold consultations with leaders of various important civil societies of their respective States and see what they can contribute towards finding solution to the protracted Naga political issue.

If the Government of India's repeated remarks are of any indication, then the issues like "sovereignty" as well as the contentious "Naga integration" have already been dropped from their agenda. Then it is generally expected that most of the serious bottlenecks have already been removed. In fact, the Government of India should have initiated the confidence building measures among the Northeast Chief Ministers and more importantly among the civil societies of the region when they knew that such bottlenecks were no more there.

Regrettably, such initiatives from the Government of India are not forthcoming and their failure to initiate confidence building measures is not only prolonging the issue but giving rooms for doubting their "integrity and honesty."

Even when 20-Member JLF of Nagaland met then Leader of Opposition in the Lok Sabha, Sushma Swaraj in October 2012 at Delhi impressing upon her for an early settlement of the ongoing negotiations between the Government of India and NSCN (IM), she was positive. She told them that ruling UPA coalition Government needed to also take the Opposition into confidence on the issue.

Swaraj, wife of former Governor of Mizoram and the first Interlocutor for Naga talks, Swaraj Kaushal, is currently Union Minister for External Affairs.

Ravi should be appreciated for his role in expanding his wider consultations beyond Nagaland in search of finding lasting and amicable settlement to the "Framework Agreement." Now his consultation initiatives in Manipur appeared to be cordial and fruitful.

According to IFP, he was reported to have told the CCM team at Imphal that it was not feasible to "divulge the details" of the "Framework Agreement" between the Government of India and NSCN (IM) at present. He, however, expressed his desire to accord "some sort of autonomy" inside the

Indian Constitution under the Framework Agreement, although the type of autonomy is yet to be settled.

CHAPTER EIGHT

SOVEREIGNTY IDEAS & THEORIES – SHARED SOVEREIGNTY & SOVEREIGNTY LIES WITH THE PEOPLE

Sovereignty is having ultimate authority over a territory, with the absolute right to govern. Thus, a sovereign State is one that governs itself, independent of any foreign power, with the full authority to make war or peace and to form treaties or alliances with foreign nations. So when sovereignty belongs to the people of the country, it cannot be shared. If it is to be shared, it is a two-nation theory or more-nation theory as in the case of European Union-Member countries.

According to Encyclopedia Britannica, Sovereignty, in political theory is the ultimate overseer, or authority, in the decision-making process of the State and in the maintenance of the order. The

146

concept of sovereignty – one of the most controversial ideas in political science and international law – closely related to the difficult concepts of State and Government and of independence and democracy. Derived from the Latin term supernanus through the French term souverainete, sovereignty was originally meant to be the equivalent of supreme power. However, in practice it often departed from this traditional meaning[1].

In the 19th Century, the English jurist John Austin developed the concept further by investigating who exercises sovereignty in the name of the people of State; he concluded that sovereignty is vested in a nation's Parliament. A parliament, he argued, is the laws and could change these laws at will. This description, however, fitted only a particular system of Government, such as the one that prevailed in Great Britain during the 19th century[2].

However, Austin's notion of legislative sovereignty did not entirely fit the American situation. The Constitution of the United States, the fundamental law of the Federal Union, did not endow the national legislature with supreme power but imposed important restrictions upon it. A further complication was added when the Supreme Court of the United States asserted successfully in Marbury v Madison (1803) its right to declare laws unconstitutional through a procedure called judicial review. Although this development did not lead to judicial sovereignty, it seemed to vest the sovereign

147

power in the fundamental document itself, the Constitution. This system of constitutional sovereignty was made more complex by the fact that the authority to propose changes in the Constitution and to approve them was vested not only in Congress but also in States and in special conventions called for that purpose. Thus, it could be argued that sovereignty continued to reside in the States or in the people, who retained all powers not delegated to the United States by the Constitution or expressly prohibited by it under the terms of the Constitution's Tenth Amendment. Consequently, the claims by advocates of States' rights that States continued to be sovereign were bolstered by the difficulty of finding a sole repository of sovereignty in a complex Federal Structure; and the concept of dual sovereignty of both the Union and the component Units found a theoretical basis. Even if the competing theory of popular sovereignty – the theory that vested sovereignty in the people of the United States – was accepted, it still might be argued that this sovereignty need not be exercised on behalf of the people solely by the National Government but could be divided on a functional basis between the Federal and State authorities[3].

Another assault from within on the doctrine of State sovereignty was made in the 20th century by those political scientists (e.g., Leon Duguit, Hugo Krabee, and Harold J Laski) who developed the theory of pluralistic sovereignty (pluralism) exercised by various political, economic, social, and religious groups that dominate the Government of each State. According to this doctrine, sovereignty in each society does not reside in any particular place but shifts constantly from one group (or alliance of groups) to another. The pluralistic theory further contended that the State is but one of many examples of social solidarity and possesses no special authority in comparison to other components of society[4].

During the 20th Century, important restrictions on the freedom of action of States began to appear. The Hague Conventions of 1899 and 1907 established detailed rules governing the conduct of wars on land and at sea. The Covenant of the League of Nations, the forerunner of the United Nations (UN), restricted the right to wage war, and the Kellogg-Briand Pact of 1928 condemned recourse to war for the solution of international controversies and its use as an instrument of national policy. They were followed by the Charter of the United Nations (Article 2), which imposed the duty on Member States to "settle their international disputes by peaceful means in such a manner that international peace and security, and justice, are not endangered" and supplemented it with the injunction that all Members "shall refrain in their international relations from the threat or use of force." However, the Charter listed as one of the basic principles of the UN "the principle of sovereign equality of all its Members."[5]

The concept of absolute, unlimited sovereignty did

not last long after its adoption, either domestically or internationally. The growth of democracy imposed important limitations upon the power of the sovereign and of the ruling classes. The increase in the interdependence of States restricted the principle that might is right in international affairs. Citizens and policymakers generally have recognized that there can be no peace without law and that there can be no law without some limitations on sovereignty. They started, therefore, to pool their sovereignties to the extent needed to maintain peace and prosperity (e.g., the North Atlantic Treaty Organization, the World Trade Organization, and the European Union), and sovereignty is being increasingly exercised on behalf of the peoples of the world not only by National Governments but also by regional and international organizations. Thus, the theory of divided sovereignty, first developed in Federal States, has begun to be applicable in the international sphere[6].

. . . .

SHARED SOVEREIGNTY AND THE EUROPEAN UNION: THE TRANSITION TO POST-WESTPHALIAN SOVEREIGNTY

The European Union (EU) has challenged many

elements of modern day politics. In particular, the EU has shown that States can come together and form a collective, in terms of sharing laws, currency, security, and other areas that are usually under the control of a singular Nation State. Consequently, the traditional view of sovereignty has especially been challenged in recent years. Since the EU is made of different Member States, in order for the EU to have power and sovereignty, the Member States have given up much of their sovereign power[7].

Political scientists have often questioned who the main sovereign in the EU is: do Member States still have most of their sovereignty or has sovereignty shifted to institutions such as the EU Commission and the EU Parliament? In reality, they share sovereignty; the Member States are still sovereign in certain areas, but have ceded sovereignty in order to belong to the EU. Furthermore, can that unique blend of sovereignty, however, fit into the international Westphalian model that exists in most nation-states around the world?[8].

In the modern world, political sovereignty without economic independence has no meaning. It is so fitting what Cuban leaders said 59 years ago. "The pillars of political sovereignty, which were put in place on January 1, 1959, will be totally consolidated only when we achieve absolute economic independence. And we can say we are on the right track if every day we take measures to assure our economic independence. Anytime that governmental measures cause a halt along this road or a turning back, even if it's only one step, everything is lost and inevitably begins to return to the more or less covert systems of colonization, according to the given country's characteristics and social context."

"We do not want to live off the sweat of others, but to live off our own sweat. Not to live off the wealth of others, but off our own wealth, so that all the material needs of our people are satisfied, and on that basis to solve the country's other problems. We don't talk of economics purely for the sake of economics, but of economics as a foundation for meeting all the country's other needs: education, a clean and healthy life, the need for a life not only of work but of recreation[9].

The idea of "shared sovereignty" to settle the Naga issue was first mooted by Pandey.

The "Federal Features" of the Constitution of India have given clear demarcation of powers between the Center and the States.

The Indian Constitution is largely a rigid Constitution. All the provisions of the Constitution concerning Union-State relations can be amended only by the joint actions of the State Legislatures and the Union Parliament. Such provisions can be amended only if the amendment is passed by a two-thirds majority of the Members present and voting in the Parliament (which must also constitute the absolute majority of the total membership) and ratified by at least one-half of the States[10].

In a federation, there should be a clear division of powers so that the Units and the Centre are required to enact and legislate within their sphere of activity and none violates its limits and tries to encroach upon the functions of others. This requisite is evident in the Indian Constitution.

The Seventh Schedule contains three Legislative Lists which enumerate subjects of administration, viz., Union, State and Concurrent Legislative Lists.

The Union List consists of 100 subjects (previously 97 subjects) on which the Parliament has exclusive power to legislate with including: Defence, Armed Forces, Arms and Ammunition, Atomic Energy, Foreign Affairs, War and Peace, Citizenship, Extradition, Railways, Shipping and Navigation, Airways, Posts and Telegraphs, Telephones, Wireless and Broadcasting, Currency, Foreign Trade, Inter-State Trade and Commerce, Banking, Insurance, Control of Industries, Regulation and Development of Mines, Mineral and Oil Resources, Elections, Audit of Government Accounts, Constitution and Organisation of the Supreme Court, High Courts and Union Public Service Commission, Income Tax, Custom Duties and Export Duties, Duties of Excise, Corporation Tax, Taxes on Capital Value of Assets, Estate Duty, Terminal Taxes[11].

The State List consists of 61 subjects (previously 66 subjects). Uniformity is desirable but not essential on items in this List: maintaining Law and Order, Police Forces, Healthcare, Transport, Land Policies, Electricity in State, Village Administration, etc. The State Legislature has exclusive power to make laws on these subjects. But in certain circumstances, the Parliament can also make laws on subjects mentioned in the State list. Then the Parliament has to pass a resolution with the 2/3rd majority that it is expedient to legislate on this State List in the national interest. Though States have exclusive powers to legislate with regards to items on the State List, articles 249, 250, 252, and 253 State situations in which the Federal Government can legislate on these items[12].

The Concurrent List consists of 47 items. Uniformity is desirable but not essential on items in this List: Marriage and Divorce, Transfer of Property other than Agricultural land, Education, Contracts, Bankruptcy and Insolvency, Trustees and Trusts, Civil Procedure, Contempt of Court, Adulteration of Foodstuffs, Drugs and Poisons, Economic and Social Planning, Trade Unions, Labor Welfare, Electricity, Newspapers, Books and Printing Press, Stamp Duties[13].

The subjects that are not mentioned in any of the three Lists are known as Residuary Subjects.

The Union Government enjoys the exclusive power to legislate on the subjects mentioned in the Union

List. The State Governments have full authority to legislate on the subjects of the State List under normal circumstances. And both the Centre and the State can't legislate on the subjects mentioned in the Concurrent List. The residuary powers have been vested in the Central Government[14].

When you say sovereignty lies with the people, the sovereignty can only be enjoyed by the citizens of that country, and then Sovereignty belongs to the people. But when the Sovereignty of the country is to be shared to end the Naga issue, it cannot be wrong to say that there is a two-nation theory trying to resolve their political conflicts through political negotiations. This is where Muivah used to elaborate on sharing competencies of the sovereignty, but his theory is different from Ravi who only said "Sovereignty lies with the people." He (Muivah), however, remarked, after signing the "August 3 Framework Agreement," "Better understanding has been arrived at and a Framework Agreement has been concluded basing on the unique history and position of the Nagas and recognizing the Universal Principle that in a democracy, sovereignty lies with the people."

Pandey's concept of "shared sovereignty" is in the areas of "Center List and State List." He explained that in some matter, States were sovereign while in some other Center was. The sovereignty in matters of State List could be further augmented keeping the uniqueness of the Naga society. "This is where we have to explore to settle the problem," he said.

If this is called "shared sovereignty," then it is, however, nothing new. It is already there. If Ravi's theory of Sovereignty that it "lies" with the people, then it is also there with each and every citizen of the Indian country. He, however, meticulously coined the phrase to avoid any undesirable debate on the sovereignty concept.

However, Pandey's open admission of the Naga people's suffering for over half-a-century due to the unresolved political issue and their entitlement to "respect and self-dignity" had won the hearts of the Naga people. He seemed comfortable in dealing with the leadership of NSCN (IM). It was easier for him to deal with them because he had earlier served in insurgency-hit Nagaland. So he knew the minds of the Naga people. He could easily hold talks with them smoothly by opening in "Nagamese dialect," which is lingua franca in Nagaland.

"I am proudly happy and sincerely believe that since both sides are coming to more understanding and sincere towards lasting solution, a solution would be found as early as possible," he replied to NEPS in January 2011. "And their uniqueness should be respected."

Nuklutoshi says that the Article 371A gives them (Nagaland) special status for "sharing sovereignty" of the country. "The Article 371A is unique which is not with any other States in the country," he opined.

Nagaland was born through a political agreement called "16-Point Agreement" signed between the Government of India and Naga People's Convention (NPC) in 1960. The Article 371A came in through the Nagaland State Act 1962. Yet, solution to the Naga problem remains elusive till today as Naga people who were fighting for the Naga cause were not taken into confidence, though some sections of Naga people said the "16-Point Agreement" was one of the finest political agreements they ever had. They, however, refused to accept it as a "final agreement" to the Naga issue.

As Constitutional complexities are expected to emerge in the course of examining the existing unique Article 371A, the idea of "Pan-Naga Hoho" or "Supra-State Body" has become a serious debate.

The Pan-Naga Hoho, according to NSCN (IM), would look after the welfare of the Naga areas not included in the integrated Nagas areas. It will be a statutory body with Executive Authority, a separate budget and negotiating power. Muivah, while elaborating the concept of Pan-Naga Hoho at the 8th Naga People's Consultative Meeting on August 25, 2015, at Chumukedima, claimed that the "formula" had been approved by the Government of India to ensure the welfare of all Nagas areas.

Sometime in last part of 2011, the parties in talks were once reported close to a settlement of the Naga issue. The final settlement envisages a "special federal relationship" between India and Nagaland

157

and the creation of a "Supra-state body" for the Nagas to "preserve, protect and promote their cultural, social and customary practices." The idea of Pan-Naga 'Supra State Body' was first offered to the NSCN (IM) by the Government of India in place of their demand of the "Greater Nagalim." So once the formula is agreed upon and as Muivah disclosed during the Consultative Meeting on August 25, 2015, at Chumukedmia, it will become a statutory body with a separate budget and decision-making power to look after the welfare of the Naga inhabited areas of Arunachal Pradesh, Assam, and Manipur. It will also have the power to "preserve, protect and promote their cultural, social and customary practices."

At a close examination of the concept of "Pan-Naga Hoho" or "Supra State Body," it is similar to the Article 371A of the Constitution of India except in the areas of "land and its resources." But the Article 371A is for the present State of Nagaland and it cannot be extended to other States where Nagas inhabit. The only option is the Constitutional experts have to see that there is no conflict between Article 371A and the "Federal Structures" of the Constitution while working out for the 'Pan-Naga Hoho" or "Supra-State Body."

The problem is such exercise will again visit certain Articles of the Constitution connected with the States – Arunachal Pradesh, Assam, and Manipur. If the Naga Integration is not on card nor is the Naga sovereignty demand in Delhi's agenda to settle the

Naga issue, the probable option left is mostly to search for a kind of "Special Autonomy" for the Naga areas of these States. It is still hazy of the idea of "Pan-Naga Hoho" or "Supra-State Body" because what type of Constitutional arrangement will be worked out to suit this plan. "Special Autonomies," which can meet the areas such as to "preserve, protect and promote cultural, social and customary practices" as highlighted by Muivah, may be worked out for the Nagas living Arunachal Pradesh, Assam, and Manipur in consultation with those States.

When the stage is set for a final settlement to the longstanding Naga political issue, all these matters will be referred to the "Constitutional Experts Committee" to study if there are any hitches that will block the smooth passage in Parliament.

And once the Parliament starts discussing on it, what will Nagaland do at this point of time? The Parliament will revisit the Article 371A of the Constitution for discussion and probably, this process in Parliament might open up the 16-Point Agreement as to how it was signed as an agreement in 1960.

Will the Members of Nagaland Legislative Assembly accept if the Parliament attempts to undo the Article 371A? The Parliament will examine Article 371A and may move for Amendment by adding some Clauses in it or by diluting it. They may try to give certain economic packages to various Naga areas but not before affecting or discussing the existing Article 371A. If they try to dilute Article 371A, then it will only create more problem than ending the issue. Again if they are trying to add more Clauses to the 371A, there will be no reaction whatsoever from Nagaland side. But again such measures will not benefit Nagas living in Arunachal Pradesh, Assam, and Manipur.

Interestingly, the Nagaland State has survived 52 years, while Delhi continues to engage in talks with leaders of Naga political groups to find a settlement to the Naga issue. The Naga sovereignty has been fundamental to the Naga political movement and the Article 371A was for making Nagaland as a full-fledged Statehood.

So, if one clearly examines the two things, the Article 371A has, precisely, got nothing to do with the Naga political issue, as the Center has been persistently engaging in ceasefires with various Naga political groups and holding talks with them to find a solution to the Naga issue. Surprisingly, the Naga underground groups generally observe the "Naga Independence Day Celebrations" every year on August 14 and strangely, all these activities go on without much obstruction from the Government side.

This is where the Government of India has also been mooting the idea of granting "some kind of autonomy" to the Naga areas in other States particularly Arunachal Pradesh, Assam, and

Manipur.

The Government of India needs to move steadily and cautiously and their "comprehensive solution" on the basis of "inclusiveness" will likely be only a political remedy if they want to see lasting and permanent solution to the long drawn out Naga political issue.

i

CHAPTER NINE

THE JOURNEY CONTINUES

INDIAN ARMY STEPPING UP OPERATIONS AGAINST NSCN (K)

CONFLICT & WOMEN – PEACEBUILDING

EXTENSION OF DISTURBED AREAS ACT (DAA) IN NAGALAND

The Naga political issue is still very unpredictable. It is so delicate and complex if one studies carefully at the nature of the issue which entangles with multi-faceted and complex ones.

Relative peace was threatened after NSCN (K)

unilaterally abrogated their ceasefire with the Government of India in March 2015. They did this after maintaining the truce with Delhi for 14 long years, and throughout this truce period, they were kept without being given any opportunity to start even minimum informal talks, whereas NSCN (IM) engaged in talks with Delhi in full swing.

It did not take long for NSCN (K) to start attacking the Indian army particularly Assam Rifles in Nagaland. However, Delhi still shrugged it off as none existent without even reacting to it. However, the BJP-led NDA Government's blue-eyed boy, Kiren Rijiju, started using highly unfavorable and provocative languages. He, however, denied making such statement after about a month.

Interestingly, the Center and its Army completely failed to judge the NSCN (K) and its fraternal ties with many insurgent groups in the Northeast till such time when the Indian army was badly attacked on June 4, 2015, in Manipur's Chandel district bordering Myanmar. In the deadliest attack, 18 soldiers of Dogra Regiment were killed and many of them were injured. This is one daring attack on Indian army by NSCN (K) in the history of insurgency in the Northeast and Delhi was woken up by now.

The incident drew worldwide attention and neighboring countries, Myanmar, Pakistan, and China, sharply reacted to the post-attack statements of the Indian authorities. Delhi alleged that NSCN

163

(K) cadres were trained by the Chinese Army. It even alleged that the outfit had unilaterally abrogated the ceasefire with them at the behest of China.

Soon after the attack, the Indian army started attacking the NSCN (K) cadres holed up inside Myanmar border. The Indian authority claimed that its Army carried out surgical strikes against NSCN (K) hideouts inside Myanmar border and destroyed their camps there. But Myanmar Government denied of such operations carried out by the Indian army. Delhi, in the meantime, started manufacturing many unfounded stories with regard to Army's operations and surgical strikes carried out inside Myanmar border after crossing the International boundary. They claimed sometimes that they could kill 100 cadres of NSCN (K), and at some other time – 80 cadres were killed.

The intelligence agencies have also been largely seen as weak in handling with many insurgency-related issues in the Region.

After three days of the Chandel ambush, the National Investigating Agency (NIA) registered the case at its Guwahati branch office and accused Chairman of NSCN (K) Khaplang of having hatched a conspiracy along with his top leaders to carry out the attack on 6 Dogra regiment convoy.

But the NIA had wrongly implicated two senior members of GPRN/NSCN (KK) group, Alezo Venuh and Kughalu Mulatonu that they were involved in the ambush on Indian Army personnel in Manipur on June 4.

Although the NIA had quickly apologized for the wrong implication of the two senior members of GPRN/NSCN (K K), they are seen having poor knowledge of the Region's issues. They have to know at least which groups are in talks and which are in ceasefires with the Government of India.

In fact, when NSCN(K) unilaterally abrogated ceasefire with Delhi in March 2015, nobody took it very seriously. Many leaders in Indian side were rather wondering when the outfit entered into a ceasefire with the Myanmar Government. Many Indian intelligentsias also felt that the Myanmar Government's entering into a truce with the outfit had indirectly undermined Delhi's ongoing truce with them (outfit). But such attitudes coming from Indian side also actually undermined the capability and integrity of the Myanmar Government.

Ethnic minorities make up about a third of Myanmar's population of roughly 50 million. They mostly live in the seven States and Divisions named after the Shan, Kayah, Karen, Mon, Chin, Kachin, and Rakhine ethnic groups. It is not only NSCN (K) that has a large presence there but there are also dozens of ethnic minority organizations fighting for greater autonomy or independence from the dominant ethnic Burman majority. The Myanmar military has been fighting with them for decades with no solutions in sight. Now look at fast development in the democratic process in Myanmar and the series of positive developments taking place with various groups operating in the country. It is only after the coming of democracy that a series of ceasefires have been declared with many of these ethnic groups.

It is nothing wrong when NSCN (K) entered into a ceasefire with the Myanmar Government as they have their large presence in the country, besides their leader, Khaplang himself is a Myanmarese Naga. In fact, it is a blessing in disguise that a ceasefire with Myanmar Government will immensely lighten the burden on Delhi. It is generally believed that the Naga issue may defy solution without the cooperation of the Myanmar Government.

■ ■ ■ ■ ■ ■ ■ ■ ■ ■ ■ ■ ■ ■ ■ ■ ■ ■

But in Nagaland, the situation is different which Delhi fails to realize. For Delhi, Indian army will be the answer to such an unwanted situation like the one happened in Manipur on 4 June. The Nagas cannot afford to allow saber-rattling between the Indian army and any Naga underground groups because they suffered enough and experienced all sort of tragedies due to unresolved political conflicts over half-a-century.

Looking at fast emerging trend in the aftermath of NSCN (K)'s unilateral abrogation of ceasefire and their subsequent attacks on Indian security forces, the Naga peace process appears to be more complex and grim. It is still very complicated as to how Khaplang will be convinced for the resumption of the ceasefire agreement with Delhi.

Northeast people do have a historical relationship with Myanmar people, besides many villages of Nagas and Manipuris are in Myanmar. It is reported that at present, there are eleven Naga MPs in Myanmar. The Myanmar army's going against NSCN (K) in Myanmar has a slim chance now after Aung San Suu Kyi's National League of Democracy (NLD) clinches landslide victory in the just-concluded Myanmar general elections. Delhi has to change its approach and needs diplomatic channels with its counterpart in Myanmar instead of asking them to flush out NSCN (K) or any other northeastern insurgent groups from their soil.

■ ■ ■ ■ ■ ■ ■ ■ ■ ■ ■ ■ ■ ■ ■ ■ ■ ■

INDIAN ARMY STEPPING UP OPERATIONS AGAINST NSCN (K)

After the deadliest attack on the Indian security forces by NSCN (K), they (Indian security forces) stepped up their attacks on NSCN (K). Their security network has been enhanced to hunt down the cadres of the outfit and started killing them on June 15, 2015, at Avakhung in Meluri sub-division under Nagaland's Phek district.

This mayhem happened when the PWC Members from Nagaland were camping in Delhi calling on various Central leaders including Prime Minister Modi, Home Minister Singh, Union Minister of State for Home Rijiju and other key persons in Naga peace talks. The PWC Members were at Delhi to give a fresh impetus to the ongoing Naga peace process. They were sharing and expressing their concerns on the fast deteriorating situation following the unilateral abrogation of the ceasefire agreement by the NSCN (K) in March 2015.

They tried their best to convince the Central leaders for the resumption of the ceasefire agreement with the NSCN (K). They also informed them of their decision to delegate leaders of Naga Hoho and ENPO to meet NSCN (K) supremo Khaplang for the resumption of the ceasefire agreement. They had even expressed their angst against the recent extension of DAA for another one year in Nagaland and strongly urged them to revoke it from the State to start confidence building measures.

So, while the PWC Members from Nagaland were having whirlwind hectic meetings with the Central leaders including Prime Minister, Home Minister, Interlocutor, Minister of State for Home on July 16 and 17, 2015 at National Capital, Delhi, the news of killing of two NSCN (K) cadres, Capt. Puhachu and Corp. Longwang, by 46th Assam Rifles troops in Avakhung and the controversial and mysterious subsequent killing of two young students, Aso (13) and Tiizali (14) , and injuring another lady Vitsiirho at Wuzu Village under Nagaland's Meluri Sub-Division created tense and highly insecure environment in the region.

The second incident, by any standard, was highly condemnable. The two minor students were shot dead at the Wuzu Village. This unfortunate incident happened when Assam Rifles troops were returning with bodies of two slain NSCN (K) cadres from Avakhung. The villagers from Wuzu Village, Phor Village and New Phor Village, after learning that one of slain cadres, Capt. Puhachu, belonged to Wuzu Village, were waiting to take the dead body from Assam Rifles troops returning with them (dead bodies) coming via Wuzu Village.

When the villagers stopped the Assam Rifles convoy in their village area requesting them to hand over one of slain cadres belonging to their village, they declined by citing certain procedures like first handing over the dead bodies to the Police who would later hand over to them. The Assam Rifles allegedly resorted to random firing probably to make their way. Two young students, Aso (13) and Tiizali (14) were killed in the firing while one lady, Vitsiirho, was injured.

Now conflicting versions were emerging with

regard to killing of two young students and the injured. Inspector General of Assam Rifles (North) Maj General MS Jaswal while talking to reporters at Dimapur on July 17, 2015, denied that the two students killed on the evening of July 16, 2015, at Wuzu Village were caused by Assam Rifles firing but they were killed due to the firing from NSCN (K) cadres, who attacked the Assam Rifles convoy transporting bodies of two NSCN (K) cadres killed earlier in Avakhung. The Wuzu villagers denied presence of NSCN (K) cadres in their village.

Terming as "bogus" the Assam Rifles' narratives of the Wuzu mayhem, NSCN (K) said the Assam Rifles deployed in the West South Asian Region were "used to harass, intimidate, butcher innocent ethnic civilians under pretext of maintaining peace during peacetime and not fit or prepared to face freedom fighters in the battle honorably." Venting their ire on the innocent public far away and long after the battle was over "shows the true unsoldierly nature of Assam Rifles," the outfit added.

The outfit condemned the Assam Rifles for what it called an attempt to "conceal hideous and horrible cold blooded murder of two innocent Naga children and injuring another civilian woman in the aftermath of July 15 incident at Avakhung village." The outfit demanded that the International Human Rights watchdogs and Amnesty International to "physically visit the spot of murder and expose before the world the decades-long Indian Government sponsored terrorism against the Naga people and entire Northeasterners."

Nagaland Education Minister Yitachu condemned the security forces for killing the innocent lives at Wuzu Village.

"Security forces are expected to maintain discipline and extreme restrain towards civilians. They must properly be sensitized with basic values of human matter of serious concern more so in the case of people living in geographically remote areas," said the Minister in a statement. He also highlighted that DAA and AFSPA was not a license for the security forces to kill and the incident at Wuzu Village had "dented the image of security forces" in the minds of the peace loving Nagas as a whole. "Security forces are expected to instill a sense of security to citizens but such actions unleash a sense of terror in the minds of the people and innocent public are left with no hope," he explained.

"Had the claim of the Indian Security Forces of the presence of the undergrounds in the village been true, the three jawans left behind by their fleeing team after the cowardly act would have been at the mercies of the undergrounds," said the Village Council Chairmen of Phor and New Phor Villages. "Rather it was because of the help from the public that the three jawans were regrouped with their team the following day."

"The claim of a failed ambush by the NSCN (K) does not arise when no undergrounds were present," they said and further stated that they did not oppose "any military operations or command by the Security Forces but will not tolerate and remain silent over the brutal atrocities committed to the innocent public."

Condemning the "blatant lie" of the IGAR (N) that the troops came under heavy fire from three sides of the Village and that the victims were killed by NSCN (K), the Village Council, Wuzu declared that "there were no armed groups whether NSCN (IM), NSCN (K), or any other groups involved in the firing." "Therefore, the question of exchange of gunfire, or shootout does not arise at all at the time of the incident in the jurisdiction of the Village or near its vicinity," said C Pitu Thur, Chairman, Wuzu Council, Wuzu.

The "Fact-Finding report" in connection with the Wuzu incident brought out by a joint fact-finding team of NSF and NPMHR had shown that the two minor students killed at Wuzu and injuring another lady were done by Assam Rifles and not by NSCN (K). The five-member joint fact-finding team had visited incident site at Wuzu Village and talked to eye witnesses from July 17 to 19 last.

Several organizations including student bodies condemned the actions of Assam Rifles at Wuzu Village.

After four months of the Wuzu incident, the Government of Nagaland has constituted a

"Commission of Inquiry" to investigate into the causes and circumstances leading to the causalities at "Wuzu firing incident" on 16 July 2015. The Commission which would be called as "Wuzu Firing Incident Inquiry Commission" will comprise of a single Member, namely Veprasa Nyekha, a retired District & Session Judge.

While the Security Forces were struggling to maintain their image and integrity, the killing of another nine people – five NSCN (K) cadres and four civilians – by 23rd Assam Rifles on August 28, 2015, at Pangsha under Nagaland's Noklak Sub-division came as a shock to many again. Pangsha is International Trade Center (ITC), some 30 kilometers away from Noklak Town which is the last village of Tuensang district bordering Myanmar.

The incident so happened when the leaders of Naga civil societies were working in consultation with the State and the Central Governments to meet leaders of NSCN (K) by crossing the International border through ITC, Panghsa. In fact, the leaders of NMA including its president Abie-u Meru and adviser Rosemary Dzivichu were about to leave for Pangsha from Tuensang when the massacre took place at Pangsha.

This incident had also come as a jolt to many people who were working hard to meet the leadership of the outfit to explain them the futility of walking away from the ceasefire agreement with India and trying to convince them to come to the ceasefire fold for the larger interest of the Naga people and solution to the Naga political issue.

Many political pundits have seen the incident as an attempt to sabotage the plan of civil society leaders to meet the leadership of the outfit in Myanmar border. However, the incident did not deter the leaders of NMA, already positioned at Tuensang to leave for Pangsha, from meeting the leadership of the outfit. They strongly condemned the killing of "NSCN (K) civilians and women" by the armed forces. They called on top officials of Assam Rifles at Tuensang and registered their strong protest against the "killings" and asked them to "exercise utmost restraint." NMA leaders also appealed the outfit to "abstain from any retaliation and give a chance for a peaceful dialogue for the sake of peace and tranquility" in their land.

Several organizations including ENPO, NSF, and NPMHR condemned the ambush by Assam Rifles at Pangsha. Expressing their deep resentment against "total disregard for human lives by the Indian Armed Forces," NPHMR said since the abrogation of the ceasefire between the Government of India and NSCN (K), there had been continuous military engagements in various forms of "attacks and counterattacks, ambushes, raids, roadblocks, frisking, and many other forms of psychological warfare and harassments which are carried out in the name of peace."

Condemning the killings at Pangsha, NSF reiterated that the ongoing political conflicts could not be solved through "military might but through dialogue." It further reminded the Government of India that regardless of factions, all Nagas were fighting for "one common goal." "Therefore, we expect the Government of India to respect the aspirations of the Naga people," it said and also appealed NSCN (K) to resume ceasefire agreement with the Government of India in the "larger interest of the Nagas and to solve the Naga political issue in an amicable and peaceful manner."

Reacting to "massacre of unarmed members" of their organization and "innocent civilians" by the Indian army, NSCN (K) said they (Indian army) should "bear the testimony before the world for generations to come that the price of the Nagas pay in blood and lives to defend her God gifted sovereign rights can never be suppressed with demonic martial forces, the sacrifices would only inflame the patriotic and nationalist spirit of the Nagas and would never go down in vain." They said, "Every martyrdom shall replicate itself and Nagas would never be found wanting in men and spirit in the fight to reclaim her birthright."

Terming as unfortunate the killing at Pangsha, Assam Rifles asked: "Should civilian lives be lost because NSCN (K) continues to operate from safe havens in Myanmar and vitiate the atmosphere in Nagaland, where people are yearning for peace?" Lamenting that NSCN (K) had carried out a number of attacks against Assam Rifles to shatter peace prevailing in the State of Nagaland, Assam Rifles asked: "Why are they roaming in uniform and with weapons in the Indian side of the border? Why are they not restricting themselves to their camps on Myanmar side where they are living comfortably after signing the ceasefire agreement with Myanmar government?"

The Indian security forces had again gunned down NSCN (K) Finance Secretary L Tuccu along with his bodyguard and another civilian. According to sources, the Indian security forces ambushed them in early hours of November 2, 2015, near Satakha under Zunheboto district.

In their latest operation, 15th Assam Rifles gunned down four Naga undergrounds but this time on mistaken identity. Later the four Naga underground turned out to be cadres of GPRN/NSCN(KK) which is currently in ceasefire with the Government of India. This incident happened on November 15, 2015 at Leangkonger Village under Tuensang district. Assam Rifles later claimed that it was an "accidental encounter."

The Assam Rifles further claimed that it wasn't aware of the identity of the cadres while the encounter occurred. They came to know later that they belonged to GPRN/NSCN(KK). But the GPRN/NSCN(KK) reacted to the Assam Rifles' claim saying that one of the victims belonging to their group identified himself as a cadre of the

GPRN/NSCN(KK) after being arrested. But instead of handing him over to the police, Assam Rifles killed him in violation of the Cease Fire Ground Rules.

....

To make things more complicated and compounded, Delhi continues to indulge in a series of double standard games. It was reported that the Government of India was quietly planning to see extradition of Khaplang for his role in creating disturbances in India. It further revealed that the Government would approach its counterpart in Myanmar for his extradition with evidences of his involvement in acts of violence in India.

The National Investigating Agency (NIA) on September 10, 2015, announced rewards on heads of Khaplang and Niki Sumi, Chairman and military commander respectively of NSCN (K) in connection with the killing of 18 Indian Army men on June 4, 2015, in Chandel, Manipur. The agency announced Rs 10 lakh reward for any information leading to the arrest of Niki Sumi, and Rs 7 lakh reward for any information leading to the arrest of Khaplang.

NIA said, "SS Khaplang is head of the NSCN (K) group and Niki Sumi is holding the charge of the armed wing of said group. They were closely associated with the decision to attack Assam Rifles personnel at Indira Gandhi Stadium, Kohima on March 26, 2015, and subsequent string of attacks on armed forces including the attack on 6 Dogra Regiment Convoy in Chandel district of Manipur on June 4, 2015, killing 18 Army personnel."

In order to make a full stop to the attempt by Naga civil society leaders to bring NSCN (K) leaders to the ceasefire fold again to find lasting and permanent solution to the protracted Naga political issue, the Government of India, after a week of announcing bounties on the heads of Khaplang and Sumi, announced banning of NSCN (K) for five years.

All these developments came in one after another as the Government of India declared that their approach to the Naga issue would be "inclusive" for finding a lasting and permanent solution.

....

CONFLICT & WOMEN – PEACEBUILDING

When we read the news of peacebuilding works by women in most violent and conflict areas of the Middle East, we realized Naga women's remarkable contributions to reducing gaps among the Naga underground groups in a land plagued with unresolved political conflicts over half-a-century.

Over the last six months, levels of conflict and political violence have risen significantly in 48 countries, according to the latest index released by global risk analytics company Maplecroft, which highlights the destabilizing effects of societally induced regime change as a key factor in the surge in risk.

Verisk Maplecroft is a leading Global risk analytics, research & strategic forecasting Company offering an unparalleled portfolio of risk solutions. Its Conflict and Political Violence Index (CPVI) is calculated twice a year by assessing the risk and severity of conflict and the impact of the violence on society for 197 countries.

According to the Maplecroft, Syria ranked top in the CPVI. This has reflected not only the severity of the conflict, which has left an estimated 150,000 dead in the last 3 years, but also the impact on its society. The country is now ranked by the Company as highest risk for sexual violence in conflict, child soldiers, and internally displaced people and refugees. The CPVI also mentioned of the sixteen countries as "extreme risk." Pakistan is ranked as 10th most extreme risk in the CPVI, Iraq (3rd) and Afghanistan (5th).

Nigeria, which is Africa's largest economy, was also rated as an "extreme risk" in the CPVI for the fifth year running, due to persistent insecurity, including increasing risks of kidnapping and piracy. The ranking of Nigeria follows the kidnap of over 230 teenage girls by Boko Haram in the north-east of the country, sparking global outrage.

"Arab uprising" in 2011 and many conflict and violence in North African countries were due to the largest upswing in risk. The countries experienced political upheaval due to societal unrest over civil and political rights and government corruption, which resulted in rising human rights violations by security forces, conflict, and deteriorating security environments.

The Arab Spring was felt in Nagaland too and it came up on the Floor of Nagaland Assembly some nearly two years back. It was a manifestation of the gravity of political situation in Nagaland as the State has been a victim of political conflicts and violence.

In all these conflict and political situations, major global institutions and women organizations have been playing crucial roles. Many internationally renowned resource persons from around the world including the United States of America participated in numerous "Conflict management and peacebuilding" seminars held in Nagaland. In the Maplecroft's CPVI, it also marked even India's neighboring country Myanmar as "extreme risk." The Northeast region has been in the map of political conflicts with Delhi for decades. Many underground groups have been maintaining a truce with Delhi. NSCN (IM) has been holding more than 80 rounds of talks with Delhi to find a solution to the longstanding Naga political problem. GPRN/NSCN (NSCN-KK) and NSCN (R) are currently in a truce with Delhi and talks are yet to be started. NSCN (K), which entered into a truce with Delhi in 2001, unilaterally abrogated it in

181

March 2015. In the Maplecroft's CPVI, India is ranked as "high risk."

The Naga mothers played crucial roles in peacebuilding among Naga underground factions ever since factional feuds broke out. Nagaland witnessed worse factional violence in the post-NSCN split in 1988. NSCN, which was formed in 1980, got split into two in 1988. NSCN (IM) was headed by Isak Chishi Swu and Th Muivah and the other, NSCN (K), by SS Khaplang and Dally Mungro.

Hundreds of cadres belonging to both the factions lost their precious lives due to factional violence. NSCN (K) General Secretary Mungro, who was a natural successor to Khaplang, was also a victim of such menace. Even after NSCN (IM) declared a ceasefire with Delhi in 1997, there was no letup in factional violence. It was after NSCN (K) entered into a ceasefire with Delhi in 2001, incidents of factional clashes came down.

The Naga publics held several peace rallies at almost all district and sub-divisional headquarters of Nagaland to register their anger against continued factional clashes. Factional clashes often took place in civilian populated areas too, and sometimes civilian causalities were there. At times, Assam Rifles also played their roles in such peace rallies.

Naga mothers under the banner of NMA organized many peace rallies in Nagaland under their famous

182

slogan "Shed No More Blood." They seriously engaged in contacting leaders of Naga underground factions with the slogan. They trekked mountains to meet NSCN (K) leaders stationed deep inside Myanmar requesting them to stop factional violence as it only brought divisions among them. The peacebuilding is complex and has multiple actors and needs creating spaces where people interact in new ways, expanding experience and honing new means of communication, says Joan B Kroc Institute for Peace & Justice, the University of San Diego in its Strategic Peace Building Principles.

■ ■ ■ ■ ■ ■ ■ ■ ■ ■ ■ ■ ■ ■ ■ ■ ■

JOAN B KROC INSTITUTE FOR PEACE & JUSTICE, UNIVERSITY OF SAN DIEGO'S STRATEGIC PEACE BUILDING PRINCIPLES ARE:

1. Peacebuilding is complex and has multiple actors.
2. Peacebuilding requires values, goals, commitment to human rights and needs.
3. Peacebuilding goes beyond conflict transformation.
4. Peacebuilding cannot ignore structural forms of injustice and violence.

5. Peacebuilding is founded on an ethic of interdependence, partnership, and limiting violence.
6. Peacebuilding depends on relational skills.
7. Peacebuilding analysis is complex; underlying cultures, histories, root causes, and immediate stressors are essential.
8. Peacebuilding creates spaces where people interact in new ways, expanding experience and honing new means of communication.
9. Peacebuilding heals trauma, promotes justice and transforms relationships.
10. Peacebuilding requires capacity and relationship building at multiple levels.

The stories of Naga women in peacebuilding were written and appreciated far and wide. One can imagine how tough their work would be in a land plagued with not only unresolved political conflicts over half-a-century but also violence and conflicts among Naga underground factions. It was a multi-pronged approach to reduce varied conflict forms which were so complicated. The Naga mothers could really soften the hardened and belligerent stands of Naga underground factions. Their roles undoubtedly worked well and one should not be surprised when NSCN (K) entered into a ceasefire with Delhi in 2001 in the midst of its rival's strong opposition.

One should appreciate the leaders of NMA for they could meet NSCN (K) leaders in Myanmar border soon after Pangsha massacre. They convinced them for the resumption of the ceasefire agreement with Delhi for the larger interest of the Naga people and solution to their issue. They (NMA) showed remarkable grit and courage guided by the spirit of genuine concern indeed!

■ ■ ■ ■ ■ ■ ■ ■ ■ ■ ■ ■ ■ ■ ■ ■ ■ ■

EXTENSION OF DISTURBED AREAS ACT (DAA) IN WHOLE OF NAGALAND FOR ANOTHER ONE YEAR

But the fact is the Center has recently extended the Disturbed Areas Act (DAA) in the entire State of Nagaland for another one year. Many criticized against the extension of DAA in the State fearing that the Indian army would again act with certain special powers under the draconian and controversial Armed Forces (Special Powers) Act (AFSPA), 1958 in the State. So the Act simply gives carte blanche to the Indian armed forces in areas declared as "Disturbed" in the name of assisting the Civil Administration.

In all these, they are immune as no prosecution, suit or other legal proceedings shall be instituted, except with the previous sanction of the Central Government, against any person in respect of anything done or purported to be done in exercise of the powers conferred by this Act.

This Act is draconian and simply an anti-democracy. This Act is nothing but a license to kill indiscriminately. This Act also fundamentally conflicts the Fundamental Rights enshrined in the Constitution of India. This Act must go and it should no more be used in this modern and civilized world. But sadly, this Act is still in force in many Northeastern States of India.

One must remember that to give such draconian power to the Indian security forces fighting against the Naga underground people, Delhi, for the first time, brought out the "Armed Forces (Special Powers) Act" Bill in 1958. The Bill was passed by both the Houses of Parliament and it received the assent of the President on 11th September 1958. Yet, this Act has become one of the most controversial Acts today in the country – drawing flak from around the world. Nagaland was like a laboratory theater for the Indian army to experiment the new "Act." Imagine the hell-bent in the 50s, 60s, and 70s when so-called a few educated Nagas had hardly realized the nature of the Act. Only after decades, people started raising the specter of it.

Now the relative peace is prevalent at least in Nagaland because of ceasefires with various Naga underground groups. At the same time, the Government of India has been holding political negotiations with the leaders of NSCN (IM) for nearly two decades for finding a permanent solution to the Naga political issue.

However, civil societies, State Government, and many stakeholders have been requesting the Government of India as well as the leaders of NSCN (K) for the resumption of their ceasefire agreement as it is also the desire of the people of the State.

While doing so, the Centre declared the entire State of Nagaland as a "disturbed area" stating that a "dangerous condition" prevails in the State and armed forces should assist the civil administration in maintaining law and order. This again gives the sweeping power to the Security forces under the draconian Act --- AFSPA.

In a gazette notification, the Home Ministry said that it was of the opinion that the whole State of Nagaland is in such a disturbed or dangerous condition that the use of armed forces in aid of civil power is necessary.

"Now, therefore, in exercise of the powers conferred by Section 3 of the Armed Forces (Special Powers) Act 1958, the Central Government hereby declares that whole of the said State to be a disturbed area for a period of one year with effect from June 30, 2015, for the purpose of the Act," the notification said.

AICC Member and former Minister, KV Pusa, also asked the Center to withdraw all black laws like AFSPA, Prevention of Unlawful Acts and also to release all political prisoners so as to remove all misgivings and suspicion among insurgent groups. He said imposing DAA in the whole of Nagaland had reflected the way the Union Government was tackling the Naga issue.

Over ten thousand students and representatives of various NGOs joined the mass protest rally organized by NSF on July 23, 2015 at Kohima demanding the repeal of AFSPA.

Zeliang and several civil societies in Nagaland expressed their discontentment and anguish over the Center's declaring the entire State as a "Disturbed area." They have demanded immediate revocation of AFSPA from Nagaland saying that DAA was extended in the entire State of Nagaland at a time when the Government, people, and various agencies along with the Central leaderships were seriously talking to find some tangible solution to the Naga political issue.

In fact, when NSCN (K) was in a truce with Delhi for 14 long years, there was relative peace in Nagaland. Even leaders of various Naga underground factions had developed good rapport among them after the FNR put unprecedented efforts for reconciliation among them.

Soon after Neiphiu Rio became the Chief Minister of Nagaland in 2003, his Government had been opposing tooth and nail to Delhi's attempts to extend "Disturbed area" in the State citing various reasons of relative peace in the State. In spite of such requests from the State Government, Delhi turned a deaf ear and announced the extension of "Disturbed area" as if the situation in Nagaland was like the 80s or early 90s. They had no compunction to the honest recommendations of the State Government.

As such, the Center's recent extension of "Disturbed area" for another one year in Nagaland was not unexpected.

Whether there is peace or violence in Nagaland, Delhi has the same mind and cannot see changes taking place in the State even after their prolonged political negotiations with Naga underground leaders and truces with them. They cannot even trust their comrade Rijiju, Union Minister of State for Home, in-charge of Northeast, as could be seen from his startling revelation that he was not aware of the Center's recent decision to declare entire Nagaland as "Disturbed area" under AFSPA.

We should also be ashamed of what the UN and Amnesty International questioning AFSPA some years back. They had even already asked India to revoke it from the Northeastern States of India saying it had no place in Indian democracy, besides it "clearly violates International Law."

It now appears that DAA may continue to be in force in Nagaland even if the Naga political issue is resolved. The leadership of the country has not realized till now that AFSPA is anti-democratic and against the very Fundamental Rights enshrined in the Constitution of India.

The Meluri mayhem and the Pangsha massacre have not only undermined the efforts of the people, the leaderships of the State and the Central Governments but have also become highly questionable because of the timing of the incidents.

This DAA under the controversial AFSPA is the problem and not the Indian Army in any way. Once the Act goes, things will be alright. It is anti-human and against the fundamental rights as enshrined in the Constitution of India.

But the "inclusive approach" for ending the longstanding Naga issue may meet some hurdles and it now depends on how the two parties in "August 3 Framework Agreement" try to accommodate those stakeholders and other groups. It is regretted that Delhi's preaching for "Inclusive approach" contradicts with their actions on the ground. The highly contradictory acts against NSCN (K) have really damaged the spirit of "inclusive approach" towards finding a lasting and permanent solution to the Naga issue.

The Indian army has been intensifying their attacks against the outfit over the last two months and even asking its counterpart in Myanmar to go all out against the outfit's bases in their soil. So it is doubtful that lasting and permanent solution to the

Naga issue will be arrived at even if they enter into any final agreement with NSCN (IM).

Their action only drives out the outfit from coming closer to them for the resumption of the ceasefire agreement, which is a single most important step for now. In fact, the outfit, in spite of maintaining a ceasefire with Delhi for 14 long years, was never given an opportunity to hold minimum preliminary political talks. Such situation actually forced them to walk away from the ceasefire agreement and now the whole world seems to turn against them for actually no false of theirs. Will Delhi do some positive exercise instead of announcing awards for information leading to the arrest of Khaplang and his army chief Lt Gen Sumi and banning the outfit for five years? Such actions are contradictory to their "comprehensive solution." It is yet to see Delhi's next moves to meet leaderships of other Naga underground groups on their formula of "inclusiveness for a comprehensive solution."

India is increasingly seen as a key global player in democracy and the world has seen how the people in neighboring Myanmar have rejected Military and voted for democracy. Myanmar's Military terribly failed to resolve many issues facing the country for decades.

After 68 years of struggles to find a solution to the Indo-Naga political problem, the parties – be it Indian army or Naga army or Indian representatives or Naga underground representatives – need to show now an exemplary maturity to the world that they can still go extra miles for a lasting and final settlement to their protracted issue. The size is not the matter. The world is fast changing and actually military concept may not be that relevant for a country's health after some years.

Precious time has been wasted on unnecessary issues. If there is a hindrance, then it has to be resolved. We have seen enough that confrontational attitudes have not worked while searching for a solution to the political issue. Such attitudes have only bred unpolitical problems compounding more to the issues. The Government of India had also failed to exploit unprecedented positive outcomes generated by FNR's consistent efforts. In fact, who could believe that members of NSCN rival factions would form one team to play soccer against a team of Naga civil societies? Who could believe that the members of NSCN rival factions would happily mingle with one another and have pleasant discussions across the table? The Naga people's crying for "unity and reconciliation" is more than their yearning for "solution" to the Naga issue. For they know that without unity and reconciliation, no permanent and tangible solution will come.

The settlement of the Naga issue demands a "political will" from a strong Prime Minister backed by a strong Government. If all his actions right after becoming the Prime Minister are to be taken, Modi appears to be straight. Yet, his knowledge to the long-drawn-out Naga political history appears to be not very deep.

But, what is "political will"? It is not just the Prime Minister takes a decision on the certain issue, but it is how he politically presents his political blueprint with a realistic political approach to the issue for the benefit of its intention, usually for the public welfare. And before any such step being planned, he has to examine outcomes from the process being presented by his Interlocutor and Representatives from the other party.

But why the solution to the 68-year old Naga political issue (some say 86 years old counting from the year Naga leaders submitted a Memorandum to the Simon Commission) still remains elusive is because their approach to solution was not with 100% attempt. Can the Naga lawmakers and the leaders of Naga civil societies explain to Modi that attempting with 80% for finding a solution to the issue which is as old as Indian's Independence will only be a piecemeal solution?

It is really complicated, but we need big hearts for big political concessions if we prefer "political will" for settlement of the "complex Naga political issue" once and for all. Time for pragmatism and not for losing the marbles!

Prime Minister Modi must learn from Vajpayee, whose genuine love, care, concern for the Nagas, and more importantly, respecting their "unique identity" changed the landscape of the Naga issue.

"I assure you that we will always be sensitive to the needs and concerns of the people of Nagaland, as also of the people of other North-Eastern States. Similarly, the people belonging to each State, and each ethnic group, in the North-East should be sensitive to the needs and concerns of their neighbors," he said while attending the "First Convocation of Nagaland University" on 28 October 2003 at the Central Secretariat Plaza, Kohima. "Let there be no doubt in anyone's minds that we are as keen as you are to achieve permanent peace with honor and dignity for the people of Nagaland. We fully respect your unique identity. It will be protected. We are proud of your culture. It too will be protected."

Modi must also learn lessons from his British counterpart David Cameron and former British Prime Minister Gordon Brown whose genuine love, care and concern shown to Scots while speaking to them (Scots) on the eve of the historic "Scottish Independence Referendum, 2014" saved the "United Kingdom" from fragmentation.

APPENDICES

APPENDIX – ONE

EXCERPTS FROM PRIME MINISTER NARENDRA MODI'S ADDRESS AT THE HORNBILL FESTIVAL AT KISAMA, NAGALAND ON DECEMBER 1, 2014

Good morning. Ladies and gentlemen, it is a great honor for me to be here amongst the friendly Nagas to celebrate the world famous Hornbill Festival. I greet you on this joyous festive season. I congratulate the Nagas for organizing this wonderful festival, which aims to preserve, promote and protect the unique cultural diversity and rich traditions of Nagaland.

I also congratulate the people on the occasion of 51st anniversary of Nagaland's statehood. On this auspicious day, I urge the Nagas that after 50 years of statehood, Look back! Introspect! And take stock of the ground you have covered so far and what remains to be achieved. I have seen the strength of your society today. A very rich cultural heritage. This must be promoted.

Your culture must not only be interpreted as your colorful dances and songs, but the Naga culture of sturdiness, honesty, simplicity, reflected in all your deliberations and actions. The Naga way of life means pride in your inherent strong character and your hard working attitude.

I also know that you have a rich biodiversity. Your region is located in one of the 25 hot bio-diversity areas of the world. This must be protected at all costs, even as your embark on sustainable development of your resources. People will come to your state for investment or tourism and they will do so because of your amazing bio-diversity and salubrious climate.

Nagaland is blessed in having a young population well-versed in the English language and in tune with what is happening around the world. This is an advantage which must be tapped. You must capture the IT outsourcing business of the world in this part of the country.

I also greatly admire the equal position of Naga women in the Naga society. I recall how smartly our young Naga women jawaans worked while deployed during the Delhi Commonwealth Games. This participation brought great pride to our nation and was a shining example for our womenfolk across the country. The contribution of half of our population to the growth of our society is immeasurable.

Nagas are sports-loving people and have the potential to perform well in disciplines such as boxing, tae kwon do, football and archery. I feel that these activities must be promoted in a systematic way to realize the potential of the people of the region, given the right direction.

I know that it has been over a decade since Prime Minister Vajpayee visited Nagaland. I think, nowadays, if I want to come to Nagaland from Delhi, or if anyone from here wants to go to Delhi, it hardly takes 10-15 hours. But Prime Ministers took more than 10 years to reach here. I assure the people of Nagaland that you will not have to wait this long for the Prime Minister to visit again. I assure you. I will be happy to come often to meet the people of Nagaland.

I will come back to see to it that everything that I have mentioned becomes a reality.

Come, let us together build a new, resurgent, stronger and more prosperous India, as well as our Nagaland.

Friends, for the last 2-3 days, I have been in this part of our country. I think it is the first time that an Indian Prime Minister has stayed in the North-East for 3 days. In India, the word "SEZ" is very popular. Special Economic Zone. But after being here for the last three days, I must say that it is not only SEZ, it is NEZ. When I say NEZ, I mean Natural Economic Zone. The other parts of India will have to find man-made Special Economic Zones. But here, Natural Economic Zones (already exist). But unfortunately, they are untapped.

It is my priority to nourish this NEZ for NE, North-East. NE is meant for NEZs. NEZs are meant for NE.

I took charge as the Prime Minister six months back. And I would like to mention some of the initiatives we have taken for the North-East in the last 6 months. I am sure that this is the right time to mention these initiatives as we are celebrating the Hornbill Festival and preparing for Christmas.

The scheme called "Ishaan Uday" is a special scholarship for students from the North-East, under which 10,000 students will benefit. The scheme called "Ishaan Vikas" will provide opportunities for internships and visit at IITs, NITs, NIFTs in other parts of India during vacation for the students of North-East. Every year 2,000 students and 500 teachers will benefit from this scheme.

We have decided to establish one modern apparel garment manufacturing center in every state of North-East. We know that we have a rich heritage in the field of textiles. We have a mastery in weaving. Our women carry this art in their fingers, and we have to utilize this capability for the development of this area. And for that, we have decided to begin with Nagaland, Assam and Sikkim. The Central Government will spend 20 crore rupees for this new program.

During the tenure of the Vajpayee government, a unique decision was taken by Atalji. It was decided at that time that 10% of the Annual Plan Budget will be spent on the North-East states. My government has made a provision of Rs 53,000 crore in the Union Budget for development of the North-East. Rs 28,000 crore will be provided for construction of 14 new railway lines. There are so many tourists here from other parts of India and foreign countries. This is the best tourist destination. All we need is road, rail, and air connectivity to develop tourism here.

Energy is lifeline. We cannot do anything without energy or power. The North-Eastern region power system improvement project has been sanctioned at a cost of Rs 5,000 crore for six North-Eastern states including Nagaland. This will strengthen intra-state transmission and distribution systems. Our goal is 24x7x365 power supply.

Nowadays, the meaning of infrastructure has totally changed. Even if you have road-rail-air connectivity, it is not enough. You require Digital Connectivity too. Under the Comprehensive Telecom Development Plan for the North-Eastern region, we have sanctioned Rs 5,000 crore for 2G mobile coverage for enhanced connectivity between this area and the world.

We have decided to establish a National Sports University in Manipur, and the people of Nagaland will be among primary beneficiaries of this sports university.

We have decided to set up 6 new Agriculture Colleges in North-East. I am sure that North-East can become India's Capital of Organic Agriculture. North-East can become a source of Organic Agriculture products for the world and for humanity.

Friends, it is a great opportunity for me to be a part of this Hornbill festival. We are very eager to develop our tourism sector. There is a tremendous untapped scope for India in this field of tourism, and we are focusing on it. There are people, even in India, who do not know what a rich bio-diversity we have in this part of India.

Seeing is believing. And I am sure that people here from different parts of India can see what a unique cultural heritage this part has. I am sure that this Hornbill Festival will improve the tourism sector of Nagaland, the people of Nagaland will be beneficiaries of this growth. And when the people of Nagaland become prosperous, the whole country will be the beneficiary.

I am thankful that the Chief Minister invited me to attend this festival. I am sure that in the next 10 days of this festival, lakhs of people will come here to be a part of this festival. Thank you very much.

APPENDIX - TWO

A STATEMENT OF DR SC JAMIR, GOVERNOR OF ODISHA AND FORMER NAGALAND CHIEF MINISTER ON THE HISTORIC FRAMEWORK AGREEMENT SIGNED BETWEEN THE GOVERNMENT OF INDIA AND THE NSCN (IM) ON AUGUST 3, 2015AT DELHI

For more than last twenty years, the common chorus of the people of Nagaland had been and still continues to be (a) no more blood bath (b) giving peace a chance and (c) honourable political settlement acceptable to all concerned. As peace eluded the Nagas for so many years – practically for more than seven decades since India's Independence in 1947; any move towards lasting peace is perceived with optimism. Viewed against this backdrop, the present Peace Accord of 3rd August between the Government of India and the NSCN (IM) has stirred the political consciousness of the people of Nagaland. That the NSCN (IM) came down from its avowed position of holding talks in a third country is an indication of it making certain concessions; and showing, at the same time, political pragmatism. We must admit that the ice has been broken. Views and opinions have been flying thick and fast, both individually and collectively, since the Peace Accord was signed on August 3, 2015. It is indeed a good sign that people are coming out openly without any reservation; commenting, analyzing and weighing different dimensions of this Accord.

However, the crux of the matter is that it is like talking about the fish without actually seeing the river. Those coming out in the open only do so knowing only the preamble of the Accord, because the real contents of it still continues to be under the sleeves. Without the full text, it is difficult or may be, unfair to make any comment one way or the other. We would venture to bring home to the readers, the political realities of any Accord whatsoever; be it an Agreement towards political settlement or a Peace Accord.

We may remind ourselves that relentless struggle by the Naga people had resulted in three Conventions. When the 16-Point Agreement was signed with the Government of India, all tribes had given their consent to it. The Nagas got a separate state for them; Nagaland in 1963, as the 16th State in the Indian Union. Article 371-A is a unique feature of the Constitution of India that recognizes Nagaland. Hence, the reality is simple: the Nagas and Nagaland function under the purview of the Constitution of India. Since the granting of statehood to the Nagas, the Government of India have been steadfastly maintaining that "Sovereignty for Nagaland is non-negotiable." Now, out of the two issues of sovereignty and integration of Naga areas, if one is non-negotiable, the other has been a complex one because "Integration" always required consensus among the concerned bordering states. Then with the statement of the Minister of State (Home) that the interests of the neighbouring states would not be hampered, only one thing is indicated. That is, the contentious issue of integration would neither jeopardize the peace process nor in any way come in the way of settling the Naga issue!

Therefore, we can safely assume that these two issues, namely "Sovereignty and integration", which have been thorns in the flesh for decades and which gave birth to fierce violent underground activities would no longer feature in any Accord or Agreement. In short, now the settlement will be finalized under the parameters of the Indian Constitution. It is not only doubtful but also nearly impossible if the interlocutor would go beyond the Constitution of the land while working out any Agreement with any group of the underground. All these political imperatives are to be considered first while commenting on the Peace Accord of 3rd August, 2015.

The other stark reality is that the people of Nagaland for whom the Peace Accord has been worked out are in complete darkness as to the exact content of the Accord. It is a bitter reality that one full generation of the Nagas has sacrificed everything to see a day when the next generation would live in peace. So when the real content of the Peace Accord will be worked out, it should take all stakeholders on board namely the people of Nagaland, all major factions of the underground and of course, the state Government.

By and large, the present Peace Accord's major achievement is the exclusion of the two contentious issues: sovereignty and integration. This indicates that at long last political realism finally dawned in the scheme of things of the NSCN (IM); the collective leadership of NSCN (IM) should now come up with new ideas to match with the Government of India's peace initiative. This is a progressive development and exhibits political pragmatism on the part of NSCN (IM). Now is the time to move forward. When other states in the Indian Union have been marching ahead, there is no reason why Nagaland and her people will continue to suffer.

A bold and forward looking Government of India is pushing for peace in the region, so that its Act East Policy will metamorphose into a vibrant reality. For that to happen, peace in Nagaland holds the key. The sooner it is understood by the Nagas in general and the underground in particular, the better it is for the state and the nation. A genuinely bold beginning has been made. Now is the time to move ahead. Now is the time for the Nagas to grab the opportunity with both hands. The younger generation of the Nagas needs to match their counterparts elsewhere in the country. Let all the Nagas unite and bury the past; and aim for one final move that settles the Naga issue for once and ever.

But then, the people should know what solution/ settlement awaits them in the contents of the Peace Accord of August 3, 2015.

APPENDIX - THREE

SPEECH BY T.R. ZELIANG, CHIEF MINISTER, NAGALAND, DURING THE CONSULTATIVE MEETING BETWEEN THE NAGALAND LEGISLATORS' FORUM (NLF) ON NAGA POLITICAL ISSUE AND R.N. RAVI, INTERLOCUTOR FOR THE NAGA POLITICAL DIALOGUE ON THE 27TH AUGUST, 2015 AT THE CONFERENCE HALL OF THE NAGALAND LEGISLATIVE ASSEMBLY AT KOHIMA

Shri Chotisuh Sazo, Speaker of Nagaland Legislative Assembly, Mr. R.N. Ravi, the Interlocutor to the Naga political dialogue, and my dear fellow legislators.

1. First of all I thank the Hon'ble Speaker, the convenor of the Nagaland Legislators' Forum on Naga Political Issue for making the arrangements for this consultative meeting between the Legislators' Forum and the Interlocutor to the Naga political dialogue. As the leader of the House, let me also welcome Shri R.N. Ravi in our midst here today. Let us hope that we will have fruitful discussions and interactions today.

2. Initially, when Shri R.N. Ravi was appointed as the interlocutor to the Naga political dialogue, there were some reservations about him from certain quarters, as we all know. However, let me say here that Shri R.N. Ravi has proved himself to be better than the past interlocutors. After having quick consultations with the Naga civil society organizations, and having a feeling of the pulse of the Naga people, he lost no time in producing the first result in the form of the Framework Agreement, which was signed on the 3rd August, 2015 by the parties to the dialogue. Let us all appreciate his style and approach to the Naga political issue. However, let us all remind ourselves that we have yet miles to go before we can relax.

3. Let us also put our whole-hearted confidence and support to the Interlocutor, so that he may be able to take forward the Framework Agreement to its final and logical conclusion. Another great asset of R.N. Ravi is his proximity to the Prime Minister, Shri Narendra Modi, whose confidence he is enjoying. He should now approach the other Naga nationalist groups, and bring them on board the Naga political dialogue. We are all of the view that the Naga political dialogue should be made inclusive now, if it is really to result in permanent peace to our land. However, without our collective efforts, and our strong back-up, he will not be able to produce the expected outcomes.

4. It may be recalled here that many of the provisions of the 16-Point Agreement of 1960 made

NARENDRA MODI AND NAGA PEACE ACCORD

between the Government of India and the Naga Peoples Convention are yet to be fulfilled. As per the 16- Point Agreement, Article 371-A of the Constitution was inserted. However, the provisions regarding acts of Parliament not to apply in the case of "land and its resources" has not been honored in letter and spirit by the Govt. of India. The Govt. of India is trying to create problems in the implementation of the Nagaland Petroleum Rules & Regulations duly passed by the Nagaland Legislative Assembly. Similarly, the provisions regarding restoration of transferred Naga reserve forests to Nagaland has not been followed up by the Central Government.

I strongly feel that when agreements are made, it should be honored and respected by both sides. This should also be the case for the Frame-work Agreement of 3rd August, 2015, and the detailed agreement that may be arrived at a later stage.

5. I hope that today's consultative meeting will provide the needed thrust and impetus to take forward the Naga political dialogue from the stage of "Frame-work Agreement" to the next stage of a detailed, inclusive and conclusive agreement, that will usher in a period of peace and prosperity in our land.

APPENDIX - FOUR

SPEECH BY NAGALAND CHIEF MINISTER TR ZELIANG AT THE CONSULTATIVE MEETING HELD BETWEEN NLF AND NSCN (IM) ON AUGUST 26, 2015

1. The Naga Political issue has dominated the political discourse of the Nagas, as well as the political agenda or election manifestoes of political parties in Nagaland during the last six decade or so.

2. It has also been the innermost desire of the Nagas for the last six decades. If any Naga is asked today what he wants to see happening in Nagaland, the overwhelming majority would most probably say- "I would like to see the final and peaceful resolution of the Naga issue".

3. With the signing of the "framework agreement", popularly known as the Naga Peace Accord on 3rd August, 2015, between the Government of India and the NSCN (IM) I believe that the Naga political dialogue has entered a crucial phase, and is closer towards its final resolution than ever before. As I am not privy to the contents of the "Framework Agreement", I cannot make any comments on its contents now. However, I feel strongly that all Nagas need to support it as a first major step towards the final

solution of the Naga political issue. I also believe that the solution should be honourable and acceptable to the Naga people as whole. I also believe that once a formula for resolution of the Naga political issue is thrashed out by the Government of India and the NSCN (IM), it should form the basis for broad based consultations amongst the Naga nationalist groups, and amongst the Naga people, before it is accepted or turned down. In my view, the most important thing now is to bring on board all the other Naga nationalist groups. In this delicate task, the Interlocutor and the NSCN (IM) may take the lead, but it will require the solid back-up and cooperation from the Nagaland Legislator's Forum, leaders of mass based Naga organisation and the church, including the Forum for Naga Reconciliation which, I feel, will need to be reactivated in order to bring about Reconciliation among our various Naga Political Groups.

4. The DAN Government in Nagaland has always been giving the highest priority to the Naga political issue. Since the formations of DAN I in 2003, we have taken several initiatives to facilitate the peaceful resolution of the Naga Political issue. Soon after taking over the reigns of the Government, the Political Affairs Committee (PAC) of DAN was formed. This PAC met the various Naga nationalist groups and had useful and wide-ranging consultations with them on the Naga Political issue.

211

5. The latest rounds of ceasefire and peace talks between the NSCN (IM) and the Government of India have also been going on for the last 17 years, since the year 1997. The State Government, Members of the Nagaland Legislative Assembly, the church and various NGOs have also been trying their best to facilitate the peaceful resolution of this protracted Naga political issue. Let me try to briefly summarise some of the significant events in the current peace process:

5.1. Resolutions of the Joint sitting of Nagaland Legislative Assembly on Naga Political Issue, made on the 26th November, 2009, resolved to appeal to the negotiating parties to expedite the peace process, and also to constitute a Joint Parliamentary Committee on Naga Political Issue, comprising of members across political affiliations, to carry the voice of House on the Naga political issue to all concerned, including the Government of India and the Naga nationalist groups.

5.2. Resolutions of Joint Legislature Forum on Naga Political Issue, made on 15th September, 2011, had given appreciation to the Naga Concordant, 2011, and also appealed to all Naga nationalist groups to participate in the process of reconciliation.

5.3. Resolutions of the Joint Legislature Forum on Naga Political Issue, made on 19th July, 2012, gave appreciation to the constructive roles played by the

Forum for Naga Reconciliation, the Church, and the civil society towards unification of the Naga nationalist groups. It also appealed to the Government of India and the Naga nationalist groups to expedite the peace process, while reiterating the commitment of all the legislators to pave the way by stepping aside from their own positions for any alternative arrangement that may come about consequent upon peaceful settlement of the Naga political issue.

5.4. In the month of August, 2012, a team of the Nagaland Joint Legislature Forum met Dr Manmohan Singh, the Prime Minister of India and various national leaders at Delhi, including the then Home Minister, Sushil Kumar Shinde, Leader of the opposition in the Lok Sabha, Mrs Sushma Swaraj, the Chairman of UPA, Mrs Sonia Gandhi and the veteran BJP leader, Shri L.K.Advani, and urged them to expedite solution to Naga Political problem. It also met the leaders of the Naga Nationalist Organisations.

5.5   All the 60 legislators of the Twelfth Nagaland Legislative Assembly, in the meeting held on 25th May, 2015, decided to constitute Nagaland Legislators' Forum on Naga Political Issue, that would carry the voice of the House to all sections, including the Government of India and the Naga nationalist groups. The Forum also resolved to constitute Nagaland Parliamentary Working Committee on Naga Political Issue consisting of representative of all political parties.

5.6. The Parliamentary Working Committee of the Nagaland Legislators' Forum on Naga Political Issue, in its meeting held on 6th July, 2015, decided to request Naga Hoho and Eastern Naga People Organisation (ENPO) to send a delegation to meet Shri Khaplang, Chairman of NSCN (K), to convey the desire and request of the Committee, as well as of the State Government and the people of Nagaland for resumption of the Cease Fire Agreement between the Government of India and the NSCN (K). It also decided to send a delegation of the Parliamentary Working Committee to Delhi to meet the Interlocutor to the Naga Peace Talks, the Union Home Minister and the Hon'ble Prime Minister to convey the need for having a peaceful atmosphere by having ceasefire with all the Naga nationalist groups, and to request them to use their good offices to settle the Naga political issue at the earliest.

6. A delegation of the Parliamentary Working Committee of the Nagaland Legislators' Forum, consisting of 19 Legislators were in Delhi from 15th to 17th July 2015 in pursuance of the above resolutions/ decisions and we met the Hon'ble Prime Minister, the Union Home Minister and the Interlocutor to Naga Political dialogue.

7. Many Prime Ministers of this country and many Chief Ministers of the State have tried to resolve the Naga political problem. Many interlocutors to the Naga peace talk have come and gone, but the problem remains unresolved. The former Prime

Minister Shri Narasimha Rao had stated that "Naga issue is a political issue, and not a law and order issue". Another former Prime Minister, Shri Atal Bihari Vajpayee had also said that the "Naga history and situation are unique". However, the main problem seems to be that the Government of India have never made an offer, in the form of a formula for solution of the Naga political problem, that can form the basis for discussions and consultations amongst the Naga nationalist groups, as well as amongst various sections of the Naga society. We impressed upon the Prime Minister and the Home Minister that it is high time that the Naga people are freed from this political tangle, and be enabled to move forward on the path to peace, development and prosperity.

8. It may be recalled here that to put an end to the violent armed conflict, which marked the Naga political movement in the 1950s, the 16 Point Agreement of 1960 was signed between the Government of India and the Naga People Convention, leading to the creation of Nagaland as the 16th state of the Indian Union. However, this did not lead to the cessation of the violent movement, as the underground Naga nationalists were not taken on board. The ceasefire agreement of 1964 broke down soon, and the Shillong Accord of 1975, instead of solving the problem of insurgency, has brought about worse situations in the State. Therefore, it is important that such kind of peace meal solution should not be attempted in the

present situation.

9. The Nagaland Legislative Assembly during its last Budget Session held last month, had also passed a 5-Point Resolution on the Naga Political issues, which was widely reported in newspapers. This resolution was again endorsed by leaders of all mass based Naga organisations in the consultative meeting held with them by the Nagaland Legislators' Forum, at Jotsama on 30th July 2015.

10. I think, we have all accepted that the Naga political issue is no more the prerogative of the Naga nationalist groups alone. It also does not belong to any particular tribe or individual. Rather, it belongs to the Nagas as a whole. It concerns all of us, because it is about our collective future. That is why we consider it necessary to have this kind of consultation meetings with leaders of Naga society. Henceforth, while talking about this Naga political issue, let us use the word "we" instead of "I". I believe, this will give the right message to our people and across the country. This way, we can move forward together without hurting each other. If we are united, and work together for a common goal, God will surely deliver us from this long struggling movement.

11. Shri Atal Behari Vajpayee, the former Indian Prime Minister, during his visit to Kohima in 2003 had said that the Naga history and situation are unique. Now, let me try to define why Naga history is unique. I think it is because we are different in:

(a) our physical appearance.

(b) our culture and tradition.

(c) our customary practices.

(d) our traditional land holding system is also different from other parts of the country

Therefore, we need to protect and uphold our own unique history and identity, so that other people will continue to respect us for what we are. If we do away with our unique culture and tradition, we are too small to be counted in this vast Indian Sub-continent. We have started with our unique history, and we should preserve this uniqueness till the end. If we stand by the principle of "one people, one vision and one goal," who can divide us?

12. In this world, leadership comes and goes. No one can avoid death. But history will repeat our deeds and achievements after we leave this world. Therefore, let us do our best to leave behind a worthwhile legacy, for which the Naga people will remember us with gratitude for what we have done.

13. This is probably the first time that the Nagaland Legislators as a group are meeting Shri T. H. Muivah and his team. I would like to thank Shri. T. H. Muivah, the Ato Kilonser who have decided to meet the Members of the Nagaland Legislative Assembly and agreed to have this interaction in this place. Let there be no doubt that we are committed to permanent peace in our land, and we will go the

extra mile to achieve this. Needless to say, peace is a requisite to development, and together, we can work towards a better and more prosperous land for the Nagas.

Kuknalim

APPENDIX - FIVE

SPEECH OF NEIPHIU RIO, MEMBER OF PARLIAMENT (LOK SABHA) ON THE OCCASION OF CONSULTATIVE MEETING ON 25TH AUGUST 2015 AT NIATHU RESORT, CHUMUKEDIMA, DIMAPUR, NAGALAND

Chairperson Mr Keviletuo, respected General Secretary Mr. Thuingaleng Muivah, Honorable Member of Parliament Mr. Khekiho Zhimomi, and honorable MLAs from the states of Arunachal Pradesh, Manipur and Nagaland, respected leaders of Naga nationalists organizations, leaders of civil societies, representatives of mass based organizations and NGOs, church representatives, tribal leaders and representatives of political parties, delegates who have come from far and near and my dear fellow Naga brothers and sisters.

1. I praise God Almighty for this significant occasion and for bringing the Naga people thus far. I thank the NSCN (GPRN) and the organizing committee of the 8th Naga People's Consultative Meeting on Indo-Naga Political talks and for the opportunity given to me to speak on this occasion. I am privileged to stand before you today as your

219

Member of Parliament to address you as a facilitator to the Naga peace process, a role our party has been shouldering when I was Chief Minister of the state and now as Member of Parliament in Delhi. I once again take this opportunity to extend my congratulations to our dynamic leaders Chairman Mr. Isak Chishi Swu and General Secretary Thuingaleng Muivah and all ranks and file of the NSCN IM for signing the historic Naga Peace Accord with the Government of India on 3rd August, 2015 at New Delhi. However, I am sad that our Chairman could not be with us today because of ill health. I wish him speedy recovery. Our congratulations and appreciation is extended to the Honourable Prime Minister of India Shri Narendra Modi ji, who has exhibited exemplary and decisive leadership in addressing the decades old Indo-Naga political conflict.

2. The Prime Minister while addressing the gathering on 3rd August 2015 after signing the historic agreement at New Delhi between Government of India and NSCN IM stated, and I quote: "Today, we mark not merely the end of a problem, but the beginning of a new future. We will not only try to heal wounds and resolve problems, but also be your partner as you restore your pride and prestige." Unquote. Moreover, during his public address in the United Arab

Emirates, he made special mention about the Naga imbroglio and the signing of the Naga peace accord, which has further internationalized the Naga political issue. All these instances go to prove that the Government of India is committed to solve the issue. Interlocutor to Naga Peace talks Mr. R. N. Ravi during his visit to Nagaland and on several occasions had stated that the Centre would reach out to every section of the Naga society to solve the Naga issue. I have also appealed to the Northeast MPs to cooperate and support our cause.

3. We must remember that it was former Prime Minister late Narashimha Rao who first acknowledged that the Naga problem is a political problem while it was during the time of Prime Minister Deve Gowda and Prime Minister I.K. Gujral when the ceasefire was formulated and declared. And then on 28thOctober, 2003, the then Prime Minister Shri. Atal Bihari Vajpayee ji on his three day visit to Nagaland stated, and I quote: "…of all the states in India, Nagaland has a unique history. We are sensitive to this historical fact." Unquote.

4. I extend my sincere appreciation to the leadership of the NSCN (GPRN) under the guidance of Mr. Isak Chishi Swu and Mr. Thuingaleng Muivah who have led the peace process and the negotiations with utmost concern for the Naga people. The fact that

the present negotiations have extended for a period of 18 years explains the difficulties which the collective leadership have endured in pursuance for the rights and identity of the Nagas. Their contributions and sacrifices will be remembered by the Naga people for all times to come. At this juncture the NSCN (GPRN) should exercise maximum magnanimity with all groups and different sections of society to foster a spirit of brotherhood and unity amongst our people. We are grateful to the civil societies, NGOs, tribal hohos, church and the FNR for what they have done over the years to keep the Naga family together and helped bring the different Naga national groups to meet, discuss and join in a process of finding a common ground that will enable the Nagas to arrive at a realistic position that is honorable and acceptable to the Nagas. The tireless effort of the FNR to strengthen the Naga reconciliation process led to the signing of Covenant of Reconciliation in 2009, Naga Concordant in 2011 and Lenten Agreement in 2014 besides many consultative meetings within India and abroad.

5. During this crucial period, we remember the contribution of our earlier leaders who have sown the seeds of Naga aspirations and carried the flame of Naga honor while protecting our unique history and culture,

despite the greatest challenges from the mightiest of forces. The Naga people owe our present status and our future aspirations to all the visionary leaders before us, beginning from the members of the Naga Club who submitted our first memorandum to the Simon Commission in 1929, to the bold, decisive and inspirational leadership of late A.Z. Phizo, and all the great sons and martyrs of our land. We salute and pay tribute to them and we rededicate ourselves towards the ideals with which they have led our people.

6. We are all aware that the 9 Points Agreement was signed in 1947 with the undivided undergrounds under the banner of NNC. However the agreement was not honored by the Government of India. Realizing the shortfalls when the 16 Points Agreement was signed in 1960, all the points contained in the 9 Points Agreement were incorporated meaning that the 1960 agreement was founded on the wisdom of the underground leaders. However, the 16 Points Agreement was signed without taking the undivided Naga undergrounds into confidence and therefore final resolution could not be achieved. In 1964 the ceasefire and six rounds of political talks resulted in deadlock and the ceasefire was abrogated. Subsequent fall out of the revolutionary government and the Shillong Accord led to

the formation of NSCN and today after 35 long years of struggle and hardship we are in the midst of the present peace process which is in pursuant of another settlement.

7. Taking this opportunity, I feel it is appropriate to recollect some of the initiatives and decisions which we have taken over the past years, in our role as facilitators of the peace process. In September 2002, I stepped down from my position as the Home Minister because I did not subscribe to the policy of the leadership and also publication of the 'Bedrock of Naga Society'.

8. With support of likeminded Nagas, we formed the Nagaland People's Front (NPF), by rechristening the cock symbol party and went to the people in the general elections of 2003 with the commitment to uphold the principles and policies of the cock symbol party, that we would play the role of active facilitator to the peace process with a firm commitment that we would pave way for any alternative arrangement that may come about from the ongoing political negotiations. On 6th March 2003, a new NPF led government under my leadership was sworn in. Our stand of playing the role of active facilitator to the peace process was a paradigm shift away from the stand of the previous government and the scenario cleared all hurdles on the home front for the

peace process and the political negotiations to work towards an honorable settlement that would bring lasting peace. During this term, despite the challenges of coalition politics, downsizing of ministry and constant defections, we overcame difficult hurdles and formed the Consultative Committee for Peace (CCP), to enhance our role as active facilitators.

9. On 3rd January, 2008 just two months before conduct of the general elections, the Government of India imposed President's Rule upon the Naga people by creating instability and defections. In our election manifesto of 2008, the NPF under my leadership committed and I quote, "The party thus stands committed to preserve the unique history, honor and identity of the Nagas. The party will also continue to play a mediatory role for any peace talk with the Centre and to pave way for an alternative arrangement in case of an honorable and acceptable settlement of the Naga political issue is found. To strive for unity and integrity of all contiguous Naga inhabited areas…" unquote.

10. Despite imposition of President's Rule, armed with our manifesto and political commitment, we returned with a bigger and stronger mandate in 2008 and formed the second consecutive NPF led DAN government under my leadership. At this

juncture we formed the Political Affairs Committee (PAC), which met all sections of the undergrounds, national workers and civil societies as we continued to support the peace process in whatever way possible within our given limitations. In continuance of our role of facilitators, we organized the first ever Naga Consultative Meet from 5th to 7th March, 2009 at Hotel Japfu, Kohima. This meet was attended by overseas Nagas and all Naga Nationalist groups, civil societies, tribal hohos, political parties and NGOs, except Congress party. The meet passed six resolutions and extended six recommendations. The DAN government followed the policy of equi-closeness in an attempt to reach out to all underground groups and bring them to the negotiating table. The need to be united in our quest for a lasting solution motivated us to change the state logo to the Mithun, identifying with Naga culture, and incorporated with the word Unity, reflecting our core conviction.

11. To further expedite the peace process, we formed the Joint Legislators Forum (JLF), which comprised of all 60 members of the Nagaland Legislative Assembly. The formation of the JLF was significant considering the fact that all members, irrespective of political affiliation and ideologies came together under one common banner for the first time, to support the

peace process under the chairmanship of the Honorable Speaker. The JLF met with all the underground groups, civil societies, hohos, former legislators and parliamentarians. We also marched to Delhi and met with the Prime Minister, Home Minister, Leader of Opposition and leaders of various national political parties. On the eve of the general elections in Nagaland in 2013, we made the clarion call that there should be no election in Nagaland till solution is achieved. All sections welcomed this move but since Congress party opposed this stand, the state was compelled to face election again in 2013.

12. We also rechristened the Nagaland People's Front to Naga People's Front and extended the political participation of our party to neighboring states to participate in the democratic process. We were faced with stiff opposition as enormous hurdles and roadblocks were created to prevent us from expanding the party. But with the support of the people and a deep sense of responsibility towards bringing the Naga family closer, we marched ahead and expanded the party to the contiguous Naga inhabited areas. We firmly believed that we were strengthening the foundations of political, social and emotional integration of the Nagas.

13. Our election manifesto of 2013 is crystal clear and I quote, "In 2003 and 2008, when

we went to the people, we gave a sacred and sincere commitment to every citizen of the state. We promised to play the role of facilitator to the peace process. We also committed that we would step down and pave way for any alternative arrangement that may come about through a negotiated settlement which is honorable and acceptable to the people. Till today, that commitment still stands. This commitment will be fulfilled on any day, be it one day, one week, one month or one year...". Unquote.

14. We won the 2013 elections with the highest ever margin of 38 MLA's in the State elections history in a democratic manner under an atmosphere of the most peaceful, free and fair election in Nagaland. Subsequently, I resigned as Chief Minister after my election as MP to the Lok Sabha. One of the predominant reasons of my going to Delhi was to work and contribute towards realization of a negotiated political settlement to the decades old Indo-Naga political problem. In the past year and a half, I have been pursuing that goal relentlessly at every given opportunity. I had spoken in the Parliament on the ongoing peace process and had urged upon the Government of India to expedite the negotiations and bring about early settlement that would be

honorable and acceptable to the Naga people.

15. The decision of all the 60 members of the current Nagaland Legislative Assembly (NLA) to form an opposition less government, in order to pursue the Naga political issue for an early settlement, is appreciated. I welcome and congratulate the efforts of the present government led by Shri. T.R. Zeliang in reviving the JLF and forming the Nagaland Legislators Forum comprising of all 60 legislators in pursuing the Naga political issue with the Honorable Prime Minister, Home Minister, National Security Advisor (NSA) and the interlocutor of the Naga peace talks in July 2015. To impress upon the central leadership to bring about an early solution of the Naga issue, the Naga Hoho and other organizations submitted a memorandum dated 12th June, 2015, to the Honorable Prime Minister and also met the Home Minister, NSA and the interlocutor in Delhi. The present hour is most crucial and we are undergoing a significant period in our history. The cry of the Naga people for permanent and real peace is now dawning upon us. This is indeed the greatest opportunity and we must all collectively make every possible effort to grab the prospect and make sure that this accord works in a successful manner. We have missed several opportunities in the past

and if we allow this chance to slip, we may never get such an opportunity again. On such an occasion I wish to place on record my appreciation of the sacrifice and contributions of all other Nationalist groups towards our cause. Regardless of their participation in the ceasefire with the Government of India, I appeal to them to join this Naga Peace Accord in order to bring about the best possible settlement for our people. I trust that they will listen to the voice of the people's desire for peace which is the prerequisite for any progress and development. It is time to act and not only talk.

16. Upholding the policy and the principles of the cock symbol party, we committed in our manifesto and as declared to the people to pave way for solution, let me assure the Naga people that we MPs are ready to step down and pave way without any hesitation in favor of an honorable solution. Even in 1964, 12 Democratic Party MLAs resigned after ceasefire was signed to pave the way for settlement. We are confident that the solution will open the opportunity for more Naga representation in legislatures and even in Parliament and therefore we will resign as MPs and we will go together to the people in democratic elections at the appropriate time.

17. The cock party, now NPF, is deeply rooted in the Naga political movement and was

formed by the founders to facilitate for realization of political solution through peaceful means and by participating in the democratic process. This is the reason why our motto is "fide non armies" meaning by faith, not by arms. The party has remained steadfast in its principles and ideology till today. Our objective has been to contribute towards a final political settlement of the Naga imbroglio and we are confident that the present peace process and the accord will make that purpose a reality. Therefore an honorable and acceptable peace accord will also mean successful achievement of the main political objective of the NPF on which the party was founded.

18. We had ventured beyond Nagaland state to nurture the growth of the wider Naga family. It is high time for Nagas to shed our differences and work together under one transformative vision of "One Dream, One Voice, One Future". Everybody should set aside their differences and pride and make sacrifices for our younger generation and their future. For this cause, many had faced untold hardships and several had sacrificed their precious lives. We are aware that for administrative convenience, the rulers divided us into four states of India, while a sizeable Naga population continues to live in Myanmar; it is our duty to seek and have goodwill of one another.

19. Nagas have to show more responsibility and maturity in anticipation of the political settlement in order to enable our society to realize its full potentials. Our society has to overcome the challenges of divisions and we must all contribute towards inculcation of a positive and responsible attitude across all sections and collectively work with far sighted vision that is in the greater interest of the present and future generations.

20. Our youth have the capability and the potential to reach the highest standards in all spheres of activity, but generations have failed to realize their ambitions due to the challenges of political conflict, insurgency, social turmoil, poor infrastructure, etc. It is the responsibility of the leaders of the present day to remove these hurdles and create an atmosphere where our children and youth also get the same opportunities and facilities like their counterparts elsewhere in the country and beyond. We must derive encouragement and motivation from the fact that despite so many challenges and difficulties, our youth have achieved excellence and success at the highest levels. If indeed we provide them with the required environment to enable them to strive for their ambitions by removing the hurdles and challenges, I am confident that they will surprise us with unimaginable achievements and success.

21. How much longer will Nagas be held back while the rest of the world is marching ahead. The time is more than ripe for all sections to come together and strengthen this peace process and create the atmosphere for our people to strive and establish our rightful place in the environments of the global village, where the parameters for recognition are success, powered by excellence. India has recognized our unique history and is willing to restore our honor and dignity. It is time for the Naga family to move forward and join the national and global community by making positive contributions for peace and progress armed with our rich culture and heritage and the vast potentials of our people and of our land.

22. Even as we move ahead, we must keep in mind that we are on the verge of moving towards an era of peace, progress and prosperity. The leaders of the day must deliver good governance with the highest integrity and combat the forces of tribal polarizations, overcome the cancer of corruption and deliver the goods that will make Nagas realize our aspiration and allow us to reach our potentials through excellence and success.

Long live Nagas – – Kuknalim

APPENDIX - SIX

SPEECH OF NIKETU IRALU ON THE 8TH NAGA PEOPLE'S CONSULTATIVE MEETING ON INDO-NAGA POLITICAL TALKS ORGANISED BY THE NSCN (IM) ON AUGUST 25 AT NIATHU RESORT, DIMAPUR

I want to thank the Organizing Committee for the invitation to participate in this Consultative Meeting today.

This is the 8th consultation conducted by the NSCN (IM). Today I am recalling the first consultation held in Niuland in 1998 to which I was also invited to participate in and given the rare privilege to be one of the two speakers from Naga Civil Society. Dr. Wati Aier was the Chairman and the other speaker from civil society.

As I prepared what I might share on that occasion a clear thought came to me at that time. It startled and inspired me. It was that the idea to consult widely with fellow-Nagas was a precious guiding thought God in His wisdom had given to the leaders of the NSCN (IM) at a very critical turning point in the difficult struggle of the Nagas for their aspirations. On more than one occasion I passed on this compelling perception to the leaders about the

234

consultation process they had launched. I said it was a fearful, awesome responsibility God had given to them because He wanted them to fulfil His plan and He believed they had the capacity to do the job.

We know Socrates's oft quoted observation that "A life not examined is not worth living." And we know from our own bitter experience over half a century now that the same thing happens to a people's struggle or movement if it is not examined and our willful human ways and schemes are not corrected to restore the health of the struggle. History is full of examples that a struggle not examined truthfully becomes impossible to pursue, and it ends up destroying itself and the people for whom it was started in the first place. And no Naga will disagree that this is true also of our "Over ground" political process. Here we must be clear the unexamined thinking and living of all of us has produced this common suicidal destructiveness.

I have believed this consultation idea was God's road map and guidance to us through the NSCN (IM) to rectify our wrong ways, and revolutionize our inadequate thinking and living so that our society will rise in unity to achieve what is right and best for all, through radical change in all of us, instead of sinking together blaming one another over who is right or wrong.

Because of my abiding conviction about the importance of this process I have decided to come again to make the same point I have been making from the start sensing that the new invitation is another opportunity for creating understanding, utilizing it for clearing up the political process that has become damaged and dirty.

At the first consultation in 1998, I said that if the NSCN (IM) starting their negotiation with the Government of India succeeded in getting India to recognize Naga sovereignty as understood by the Naga people, the entire Naga public and all the rival groups would simply say "Thank you" and get on to celebrate the achievement together. But if they discovered that Delhi was not in a position to discuss sovereignty because it was too difficult for India, and IM decided to negotiate for something other than sovereignty, they needed to call the different fragmented groups and tell them the truth about the new situation and thrash out together in complete transparency a common position on the terms for political negotiations with Delhi for a settlement of the Indo-Naga issue.

And today I emphasize that you consult and take into consideration the views of all the other factions even if you don't agree with all their points. Failing to do this, history will always judge and things, as you know better, can go very wrong. This would also be the beginning of real reconciliation as this would be deciding together honestly on the most difficult issue over which Nagas have killed Nagas and the Indian Army has killed Nagas and all Nagas have paid a very heavy price of suffering. I recall saying on that occasion that, given the hurts we had inflicted on one another already, without honesty with one another at this level, distrust and resentment would take over and our society would head for disaster.

It will be fair to say that the vast majority of the public yearn for the consultation process to achieve the most desired unity and mutual goodwill and cooperation among our national workers. And because of the undoubted potential of consultation to achieve a desperately needed miracle for our people in our worsening crisis, allow me to make this plea even now that as part of your continuing consultations a very special invitation be extended to the different groups of the struggle to come together and they are told the envisaged details of the agreement being pursued with the Government of India. This would be a telling gesture that will speak loudly and may do unexpected good things to the process.

Finally, the deepest fear and concern with which our people are wrestling is what will happen after a settlement. The greatest gift the NSCN (IM) and the Government of India can give to the Nagas is to guarantee that no violence or threat of violence will be employed in the implementation of whatever settlement may emerge. No one yet knows what the details of the agreement are going to be. All is speculation so far. The hope and deepest desire of our people is that when it comes it will take our society and whole region forward so that a stability hitherto unknown will become a reality and growth and development in all dimensions will become possible.

I would like to end with 4 points a friend I met and consulted yesterday asked me to express today. They were made by Bill Clinton on a visit to Wales concerning Conflict Resolution:

1. Present day problems are mostly the fear of the other.
2. The need of the day is to think of a future different from the past.
3. No one has the monopoly of the truth.
4. To befriend a people, you have to understand not only their dreams and hopes, but also understand their worst nightmares.

The Nagas have gone through terrible nightmares. Whatever any settlement any group may bring, nightmares on no account should be the consequence for the people anymore.

APPENDIX - SEVEN

MEMORANDUM SUBMITTED TO PRIME MINISTER, NARENDRA MODI, BY NAGALAND LEGISLATORS FORUM (NLF) WHILE MEETING HIM ON 17 JULY 2015 AT DELHI

1.   The peaceful resolution of the more than six decade old Naga political issue has always been the topmost priority of successive State Governments of Nagaland since it attained statehood in 1963. It is also at the core of the yearnings and desires of the people of Nagaland. Ever since India's independence, several rounds of talks between the Government of India and the Naga nationalist groups had been held for more than 60 years but without any substantive outcome. The latest rounds of ceasefire and peace talks between the NSCN(IM) and the Government of India have also been going on for the last 17 years, since the year 1997, without any conclusion. The State Government, Members of the Nagaland Legislative Assembly, the church and various NGOs have also been trying their best to facilitate the peaceful resolution of this protracted Naga political issue. Some of the significant events in the current peace process are recapitulated below:-

1.1. The Covenant of Reconciliation, 2009 was

signed by Shri Isak Chishi Swu, Chairman of NSCN (IM), Shri S.S. Khaplang, Chairman, NSCN (K) and Brig (Rtd.) S. Singnya, President, FGN/ NNC wherein the three main Naga nationalist groups decided to work together for the common Naga political cause. The covenant was signed under the auspices of the Forum for Naga Reconciliation formed by various church leaders.

1.2. Resolutions of the Joint sitting of Nagaland Legislative Assembly on Naga Political Issue, made on the 26th November, 2009, resolved to appeal to the negotiating parties to expedite the peace process, and also to constitute a Joint Parliamentary Committee on Naga Political Issue, comprising of members across political affiliations, to carry the voice of House on the Naga political issue to all concerned, including the Government of India and the Naga nationalist groups.

1.3. The Naga Concordant, 26th August, 2011 was signed by the top leaders of the three main Naga nationalist groups, NSCN (IM), NSCN (K) and FGN/NNC, wherein they resolved to work towards unity and towards formation of one Naga nationalist organisation.

1.4. Resolutions of Joint Legislature Forum on Naga Political Issue, made on 15th September, 2011, had given appreciation to the Naga Concordant, 2011, and also appealed to all Naga nationalist groups to participate in the process of reconciliation.

1.5. Resolutions of the Joint Legislature Forum on Naga Political Issue, made on 19th July, 2012, gave appreciation to the constructive roles played by the Forum for Naga Reconciliation, the Church, and the civil society towards unification of the Naga nationalist groups. It also appealed to the Government of India and the Naga nationalist groups to expedite the peace process, while reiterating the commitment of all the legislators to pave the way by stepping aside from their own positions for any alternative arrangement that may come about consequent upon peaceful settlement of the Naga political issue.

1.6. In the month of August, 2012, a team of the Nagaland Joint Legislature Forum met Dr Manhmohan Singh, the Prime Minister of India and various national leaders at Delhi, including the then Home Minister, Sushil Kumar Shindhe, Leader of the opposition in the Lok Sabha, Mrs Sushma Swaraj, the Chairman of UPA, Mrs Sonia Gandhi and the veteran BJP leader, Shri L.K. Advani, and urged them to expedite the Naga peace process. It also met the leaders of the Naga nationalist organizations.

1.7. All the 60 legislators of the Twelfth Nagaland Legislative Assembly, in their meeting held on 25th May, 2015, decided to constitute Nagaland Legislators' Forum on Naga Political Issue, that would carry the voice of the House to all sections, including the Government of India and the Naga nationalist groups. The Forum also resolved to constitute Nagaland Parliamentary Working Committee on Naga Political Issue consisting of representative of all political parties.

1.8. The Parliamentary Working Committee of the Nagaland Legislators' Forum on Naga Political Issue, in its meeting held on 6th July, 2015, decided to request Naga Hoho and Eastern Naga People Organization (ENOP) to send a delegation to meet Shri Khaplang, Chairman of NSCN (K), to convey the desire and request of the Committee, as well as of the State Government and the people of Nagaland for resumption of the Cease Fire Agreement between the Government of India and the NSCN (K). It also decided to send a delegation of the Parliamentary Working Committee to Delhi to meet the Interlocutor to the Naga Peace Talks, the Union Home Minister and the Hon'ble Prime Minister to convey the need for having a peaceful atmosphere by having ceasefire with all the Naga nationalist groups, and to request them to use their good offices to settle the Naga political issue at the earliest.

2. A delegation of the Parliamentary Working Committee of the Nagaland Legislators' Forum, consisting of 23 Legislators (including the two MPs of Nagaland) has come to Delhi on 15th July 2015 in pursuance of the above resolutions/ decisions to meet the Interlocutor to Naga peace talk, the Union Home Minister, and the Hon'ble Prime Minister and other national leaders.

3.   It may also be recalled here that to put an end to the violent armed conflict, which marked the Naga political movement in the 1950s, the 16 Point Agreement of 1960 was signed between the Government of India and the Naga People Convention, leading to the creation of Nagaland as the 16th state of the Indian Union. However, this did not lead to the cessation of the violent movement, as the underground Naga nationalists were not taken on board. The ceasefire agreement of 1964 broke down soon, and the Shillong Accord of 1975, instead of solving the problem of insurgency, has brought about worse situations in the State. Therefore, we feel that such kind of peace meal solution should not be attempted in the present situation.

4.   When the people of the state expresses desire for peace, declaring the entire state of Nagaland as disturbed area under the Armed Forces Special Power Act vitiate the peaceful atmosphere necessary for a peaceful resolution to the Naga people problem. Therefore, declaration of the whole of Nagaland State as disturbed area under the AFSP Act should be lifted for the sake of confidence building amongst the Naga people and to facilitate early solution of the Naga political problem.

5.   Many Prime Ministers of this country and many Chief Ministers of the State have tried to resolve the Naga political problem. Many interlocutors to the Naga peace talk have come and gone, but the problem remains unresolved. The

former Prime Minister Shri Narasimha Rao had stated that "Naga issue is a political issue and not a law and order issue". Another former Prime Minister, Shri Atal Bihari Vajpayee had also said that the "Naga history and situation are unique". However, the main problem seems to be that the Government of India have never made an offer, in the form of a formula for solution of the Naga political problem, that can form the basis for discussions and consultations amongst the Naga nationalist groups, as well as amongst various sections of the Naga society. We also believe that it is high time that the Naga people are freed from this political tangle, and be enabled to move forward on the road to peace, development and prosperity.

6. The Nagaland Legislators' Forum, the Government of Nagaland, the civil societies and the people of Nagaland have high hopes and confidence on the dynamic leadership of the Hon'ble Prime Minister of India, Shri Narendra Modi, to amicably resolve the long pending Naga political issue to bring about permanent and lasting peace in Nagaland, that would be a befitting tribute to the statesmanship of Shri Narendra Modi, the Hon'ble Prime Minister of India.

APPENDIX - EIGHT

NAGA CLUB MEMORANDUM SUBMITTED TO SIMON COMMISSION

Dated, 10 January, 1929

To

**The British Statutory Commission;
Camp-India**

Subs: Memorandum of the Naga Hills

Sir,

We the Undersigned Nagas of the Naga Club at Kohima, who are the only persons at present who can voice for our people have heard with great regret that our Naga Hills is included in the Reformed Scheme of India without our knowledge, but as administration of our Hills is continued to be in the hands of the British Officers and we did not consider it necessary to raise any protest in the past. Now we learnt that you have come to India as representative of the British Government to enquire into the working of the system of Government and the growth of education and we beg to submit below our view with prayer that our Hills may be withdrawn from the Reformed Scheme and placed outside the Reforms but directly under British Government. We never asked for any reforms and we do not wish for any reforms.

Before the British Government conquered our country in 1879-80, we were living in a state of intermitted warfare with the Assamese of the Assam valley to the North and West of our country and Manipuris to the South. They never conquered us nor were we subjected to their rules. On the other hand, we were always a terror to these people. Our country within the administered area consists of more than eight regions quite different from one another, with quite different languages which cannot be understood by each other, and there are more regions outside the administered area which are not known at present. We have no unity among us and it is only the British Government that is holding us together now.

Our education is poor. The occupation of our country by the British Government being so recent as 1880, we have had no chance or opportunity to improve in education and though we can boast of two three graduates of an Indian University in our country, we have not got one yet who is able to represent all our different regions or master our languages much less one to represent us in any council of a province. Moreover, our population numbering 1, 02,000 is very small in comparison with the population of the plain district in the province; and any representation that may be allotted to us in the council will be negligible and will have no weight whatever. Our language is quite different from those of the plains and we have no social affinities with the Hindus or Mussalmans. We are looked down upon by the one for "beef" and the other for our "pork" and by both for our want in education, is not due to any fault of ours.

Our country is poor and it does not pay for any administration. Therefore if it is continued to be placed under Reformed Scheme, we are afraid new and heavy taxes will have to be imposed on us, and when we cannot pay, then all lands have to be sold and in long run we shall have no share in the land of our birth and life will not be worth living then. Though our land at present is within the British territory, Government have always recognized our private rights in it, but if we are forced to enter the council the majority of whose number is sure to belong to other districts, we also have much fear the introduction of foreign laws and customs to supersede our own customary laws which we now enjoy.

For the above reasons, we pray that the British Government will continue to safeguard our rights against all encroachment from other people who are more advanced than us by withdrawing our country that we should not be thrust to the mercy of other people who could never be subjected; but to leave us alone to determine ourselves as in ancient times. We claim not only the members of "Naga Club" to represent all those regions to which we belong viz, Angamis, Kacha Nagas, Kukis, Semas, Lothas and Rengmas, but also other regions of Nagaland.

Signed by
(1) Nihu Angami, Head Interpreter,
(2) Hisale Peshkar,
(3) Nisier Angami, Master,
(4) Khosa Doctor,
(5) Gebo Kacha Nagas, Interpreter,
(6) Vipunyu Angami, Potdar
(7) Goyiepra Angami, Treasurer,
(8) Ruzhukhrie Angami, Master,
(9) Dikhrie Angami, Sub-overseer,
(10) Zapuzhulie Angami, Master,
(11) Zapulie Angami, Interpreter,
(12) Katsuno Angami, Interpreter,
(13) Nuolhoukielie Angami, Interpreter,
(14) Inzevi Sema, Interpreter,
(15) Apamo Lotha, Interpreter,
(16) Resile Rengma, Interpreter,
(17) Lengjang Kuki, Interpreter,
(18) Neikhriehu Angami, Interpreter,
(19) Miakrao Angami, Chaprasi,
(20) Levi Kacha Naga, Clerk.

APPENDIX - NINE

THE NAGA-AKBAR HYDARI ACCORD, 1947

Tribes Represented at Discussions on the 26th, 27th and 28th June, 1947 at Kohima

Western Angamis, Eastern Angamis, Kukis, Kacha Nagas (Mzemi), Rengmas, Semas, Lotha, Aos, Sangtams, Changs.

Heads of Proposed Understanding

That the right of the Nagas to develop themselves according to their freely expressed wishes is recognized.

1. Judicial – All cases whether civil or criminal arising between Nagas in the Naga Hills will be disposed of by duly constituted Naga Courts according to Naga customary law or such law as may be introduced with the consent of duly recognized Naga representative organizations: save that where a sentence of transportation or death has been passed there will be a right of appeal to the Governor.

In cases arising between Nagas and non-Nagas in (a) Kohima and Mokokchung town areas, and (b) in the neighbouring plains districts, the judge if not a Naga will be assisted by a Naga assessor.

2. Executive – The general principle is accepted that what the Naga Council is prepared to pay for, the Naga Council should control. This principle will apply equally to the work done as well as the staff employed. While the District Officer will be appointed at the discretion of the Governor, Subdivisions of the Naga Hills should be administered by a Subdivisional Council with a full time executive President paid by Naga Council who would be responsible to the District Officer for all matters falling within the latter's responsibility, and to the Naga Council for all matters falling within their responsibility.

In regard to:
(a) Agriculture – the Naga Council will exercise all the powers now vested in the District Officer.
(b) C.W.D. – The Naga Council would take over full control. (c) Education and Forest Department – The Naga Council is prepared to pay for all the services and staff.

3. Legislative – That no laws passed by the Provincial or Central Legislature which would materially affect the terms of this agreement or the religious practices of the Nagas shall have legal force in the Naga Hills without the consent of the Naga Council. In cases of dispute as to whether any law did so affect this agreement the matter would be referred by the Naga Council to the Governor who would then direct that the law in question should not have legal force in the Naga Hills pending the decision of the Central Government.

4. Land – That land with all its resources in the Naga Hills should not be alienated to a non-Naga without the consent of the Naga Council.

5. Taxation – That the Naga Council will be responsible for the imposition, collection, and expenditure of land revenue and house tax and of such other taxes as may be imposed by the Naga Council.

6. Boundaries – That present administrative divisions should be modified so as

(1) to bring back into the Naga Hills District all the forests transferred to the Sibsagar and Nowgong Districts in the past, and

(2) to bring under one unified administrative unit as far as possible all Nagas. All the areas so included would be within the scope of the present proposed agreement. No areas should be transferred out of the Naga Hills without the consent of the Naga Council.

7. Arms Act – The Deputy Commissioner will act on the advice of the Naga Council in accordance with the provisions of the Arms Act.

8. Regulations – The Chin Hills regulations and the Bengal Eastern Frontier Regulations will remain in force.

9. Period of Agreement – The Governor of Assam as the Agent of the Government of the Indian Union will have a special responsibility for a period of 10 years to ensure the observance of the agreement, at the end of this period the Naga Council will be asked whether they require the above agreement to be extended for a further period or a new agreement regarding the future of Naga people arrived at.

APPENDIX - TEN

THE SHILLONG ACCORD OF 11 NOVEMBER 1975

BETWEEN THE GOVERNMENT OF INDIA AND THE UNDERGROUND NAGAS

The following representatives of the underground organizations met the Governor of Nagaland, Shri L.P. Singh, representing the Government of India, at Shillong on 10 and 11 November 1975.

1.

(a) Shri I. Temjenba, (b) Shri Dahru, (c) Shri Venyiyi Rhakhu, (d) Shri Z. Ramyo, (e) Shri M. Assa, (f) Shri Kevi Yallay

2. There was a series of four discussions. Some of the discussions were held with the Governor alone; at others, the Governor was assisted by the two Advisers for Nagaland, Shri Ramunny and Shri H. Zopianga, and Shri M.L. Kampani, Joint Secretary in the Ministry of Home Affairs. All the five members of the Liaison Committee namely Rev. Longri Ao, Dr. M. Aram, Shri L. Lungalang, Shri Kenneth Kerhuo and Shri Lungshim Shaiza, participated in the discussions.

3. The following were the outcome of the

253

discussions:

i. The representative of the underground organizations conveyed their decision on their own volition, to accept without condition, the Constitution of India;

ii. It was agreed that the arms, now underground, would be brought out and deposited at appointed places. Details for giving effect to this agreement will be worked out between them and the representatives of the government, the security forces and the members of the Liaison Committee;

iii. It was agreed that the representatives of the underground organizations should have reasonable time to formulate other issues for discussion for final settlement.

Dated Shillong: 11 November 1975

Sd/-　**I Temjenba**
Sd/-　**S. Dehru**
Sd/-　**Z. Ramyo**
Sd/-　**M. Assa**
Sd/-　**Kevi Yallay**

(On behalf of the representatives of underground organizations)

Sd/-　L.P. Singh

(On behalf of the Government of India)

SUPPLEMENTARY AGREEMENT TO THE SHILLONG ACCORD WAS SIGNED AGAIN ON 5 JANUARY 1976 FOR IMPLEMENTATION OF CLAUSE 2 OF THE SHILLONG ACCORD OF 11 NOVEMBER 1975:

1. It was decided that the collection of arms initially at collection centers would commence as early as possible and will be completed by 25 January 1976. Initially, places of collection to be decided through discussion between the Commissioner, representatives of underground organizations and the members of the Liaison Committee.
2. Once all the arms are collected, these will be handed over to the Peace Council Team at the respective places of collection.
3. The Peace Council Team will arrange to transport the arms from collection centers of Chedema Peace Camp and to arrange guards etc. for safe custody of the arms.
4. Similar arrangement at agreed place(s) will be made in Manipur with the concurrence of the Manipur Government.
5. The underground may stay at Peace Camps to be established at suitable places and only the Peace Council will arrange their maintenance. Any voluntary contribution from any source will be made to the Peace

Council, which will utilize the fund according to necessity.

Dated Shillong: 5 January 1976

APPENDIX - ELEVEN

SPEECH BY NIKETU IRALU ON THE OCCASION OF THE 8TH NAGA UNIFICATION ANNIVERSARY HELD AT GPRN/NSCN (NSCN-KK) KHEHOI CAMP ON 22 NOVEMBER 2015.

I have attended consultations for building understanding and anniversary events called by the different political groups of the Naga struggle during the past 25 years or so. I have appreciated the invitations to the events as I do appreciate in equal measure the invitation to this event also today. I want to thank the collective leadership of GPRN/NSCN (NSCN-KK) for giving me this opportunity.

The Naga struggle for our aspirations for identity and dignity launched by our pioneers was and is right. It was not at all against India or Burma/Myanmar our neighbors. It was our considered decision to claim our identity and our rightful political status as a people and a nation as fully justified by the facts our history and geography, as our elders of the day understood. We made our position abundantly clear in writing before the British left their empire in South Asia.

The Nagas have fought with heroism ever since for the past seventy years showing that that they meant what they had said. The Naga struggle therefore is not an illegal movement for secession from India and Burma, violating agreements made earlier for union - unlike the other movements and struggles that erupted in different parts of India after the British left.

The struggle represents the response of the Nagas to the unprecedented changes that had come to impact them in their isolated homeland in the interior of Asia.

But the struggle to become a people and to grow as a nation is the most demanding and complicated venture for any people to start and pursue. In all such struggles the people involved make all kinds of mistakes because of the weaknesses and shortcomings common to all human beings. We the Nagas too have made serious mistakes. And let us not forget we are just at the beginning of our story.

What we are meant to do is to learn from our mistakes by maturely and responsibly acknowledging where we have gone wrong. Our crisis today is threatening to overwhelm us because instead of admitting our own mistakes, which will inspire others to do likewise, we are blaming one another and this has paralyzed our struggle and our society. This short-sighted, suicidal folly is provoking the worst, the meanest out of all Nagas. It has brought us to a dead end.

This occasion today is a crucial moment when we together should discover the common meeting ground where we are all the same before our Creator. I am talking about the soul and conscience inside each one of us. It is the core essence of our personality and our only dependable guide for restoration of trust and unity that will enable us to survive and succeed today. Conscience is the truest friend of all of us no matter which faction, tribe or party we may belong to.

Listening to our head only in the conduct of our politics and economic development has produced clever tactics and stratagems against one another. The problems that have resulted from this have become too heavy a burden for our people to bear. Let no group, faction or tribe underestimate the anger and the despair now in the hearts of our people. The time has come when we must all listen to the conscience that is inside all of us to find our way out of the dead-end we have come to.

From our conscience will come imaginative, constructive ideas of statesmanship that will be right for all Nagas. It is said "Statesmanship is doing today what events will force you to do tomorrow". This kind of statesmanlike leadership is what we urgently need from the leaders of all groups and factions today. Anything less will keep us in endless distrust and vengeful bitterness against one another. We all know we cannot achieve anything lasting if mutual distrust will be allowed to continue to paralyze us and keep us selfish and tribe-centered.

We are entering a new year and a new situation where all Nagas of all tribes, factions and parties must take a united solemn pledge that that no faction or tribe will use violence and force to gain their own advantage at the expense of others. Nagas will no longer allow the darkness of hatred and violence that they have endured to return. The Government of India engaged in ceasefire and negotiation talks with various groups will be held equally responsible if violence and force will be used to implement any settlement and let the Nagas continue to suffer.

I shall end with these questions:

Did God make a mistake when He made Nagas into so many tribes?

Did He make another mistake when He gave to all Naga tribes the common desire to be a people and a nation? There is no doubt it has become extremely difficult today to go forward together. I believe God did not make a mistake. But He gave us a most difficult assignment because He has a very difficult and important role for us to play as a bridge people in a region of Asia where some very ancient civilizations and great nations and cultures meet. I believe we will learn to play our role because He gave it to us obviously trusting us to rise to it.

APPENDIX - TWELVE

THE 16 POINTS TO FORM THE BASIS OF NEGOTIATION FOR THE NAGA POLITICAL SETTLEMENT

1. **The Name:-**

   The territories that were here-to-fore known as the Naga Hills-Tuensang Area under the Naga Hills-Tuensang Area Act 1957, and any other Naga area, which may hereafter come under it, shall form a State within the Indian Union and be hereafter known as Nagaland.

2. **The Ministry In-charge:-**

   The Nagaland shall be under the Ministry of External Affairs of the Government of India.

3. **The Governor:-**

   i. The President of India shall appoint a Governor for Nagaland and he will be vested with the Executive Powers of the Government of Nagaland, and he will function from the Headquarters of the Nagaland.

   ii. His administrative secretariat will be headed by a Chief Secretary stationed at the Headquarters with other Secretariat Staff as necessary.

   iii. The Governor shall have special responsibility with regard to Law,

Order and Police during transitional period only.

4. **Council of Ministers:-**

    i. There shall be a Council of Ministers (viz. Six Ministers and Three Deputy Ministers) with a Chief Minister at the head to assist and advise the Governor in the exercise of his functions.

    ii. The Council of Ministers shall be responsible to the Naga Legislative Assembly.

5. **The Legislature:-**

    There shall be constituted a Legislative Assembly consisting of elected and nominated members as may be deemed necessary representing different Tribes. (Further, a duly constituted body of Experts may be formed to examine and determine the principles of representation on democratic basis).

6. **Representation in the Parliament:-**

    Three elected members shall represent the Nagaland in the Union Parliament, that is, two in the Lok Sabha and one in the Rajya Sabha.

7. **Acts of Parliament:-** No Acts or Law passed by the Union Parliament affecting the following provisions shall have legal force in Nagaland unless specifically applied to it by a majority vote of the Naga Legislative Assembly:

      i. The Religious or Social practices of the Nagas.

      ii.   Naga Customary Laws and Procedure.

      iii.   Civil and Criminal Justice so far as these concern decisions according to Naga Customary Laws.

      iv.   The ownership and transfer of land and its resources.

8. **Local Self-Government:-** Each tribe shall have the following Units of Law-making and Administrative Local Bodies to deal with matters concerning the respective tribes and areas:

      i. The Village Council.

      ii.   The Range Council.

      iii.   The Tribal Council.

9. **Administration of Justice:-**

    a.   Each tribe shall have the following Courts of Justice:-

      i. Village Court.

      ii. The Range Court.

      iii.   The Tribal Court.

    b.   Appellate Courts:-

      i. The District Court-cum-Session Court (for each District), and Supreme Court of India.

      ii. The Naga Tribunal (for the whole of the Nagaland) in respect of cases decided according to Customary Law.

10. **Administration of Tuensang District:-**

i. The Governor shall carry on the administration of the Tuensang District for a period of ten (10) years until such time when the tribes in the Tuensang District are capable of shouldering more responsibilities of the advance system of administration. The commencement of the ten years period of administration. The commencement of the ten-year period of administration will start simultaneously with enforcement of detailed workings of Constitution in the other parts of the Nagaland.

ii. Provided further that a Regional Council shall be formed for Tuensang District by elected representative from all the Tribes in Tuensang District, and the Governor may nominate representatives to the Regional Council as well. The Deputy Commissioner will be the ex-officio Chairman of the Council. This Regional Council will elect members to the Naga Legislative Assembly to represent Tuensang District.

iii. Provided further that on the advice of the Regional Council, steps will be taken to start various Councils and Courts in those areas where the people feel themselves capable of establishing such institutions.

iv.   Provided further that no Act or Law passed by the Naga Legislative Assembly shall be applicable to Tuensang District unless specifically recommended by the Regional Council.

v.   Provided further that the Regional Council shall supervise and guide the working of the various Councils and Courts within Tuensang District and wherever deem necessary the dispute the Local Officers to act as Chairman thereof.

vi.   Provided further that Councils of such areas inhabited by a mixed population or which have not as yet decided to which specific tribal Council to be affiliated to, shall be directly under the Regional Council for the time being. And at the end of ten years the situation will be reviewed and if the people so desired the period will be further extended.

11. **Financial Assistance from the Government of India:-**

To supplement the revenues of the Nagaland, there will be a need for the Government of India pay out of the Consolidated Fund of India as Grants-in-aid as follows:-

  i. Lump-sums as may be necessary each year for the development program in the Nagaland.

  ii. A fixed recurring sum (Annual Subvention) for meeting the cost of the administration of Nagaland.

12. All the Reserved Forests and other Naga areas that were transferred out of Naga areas will be returned to the Nagaland with a clearly defined boundary under the present settlement.

13. **Consolidation of Contiguous Naga Area:-** The other Naga Tribes inhabiting the areas contiguous to the present Nagaland should be allowed to join the Nagaland if they so desire.

14. **Formation of Separate Naga Regiment:-** In order that Naga people can fulfill their desire of playing a full role in the defence forces of India, the question of raising a separate Naga Regiment should be duly examined for action.

15. **Transitional Period:-**
  i. On reaching the political settlement with the Government of India, the Naga People's Convention shall appoint a Body to draft the detail of the Constitution for the Nagaland on the basis of the settlement.

  ii. There shall be constituted an Interim Body with elected representatives from every tribe, to assist and advice

266

the Governor in the Administration of the Nagaland during the transitional period. The tenure of office of the members of the Interim Body will be 3 (three) years subject to re-election.

16. Inner Line Regulation:-

Rules embodied in the Protected Area.

Act of 1958 shall remain in force in the Nagaland.

Sd/-
(Dr. Imkongliba Ao)
President
Naga People's Convention

Sd/-
(Vizol)
Vice President

Sd/-
(Jasokie)
Secretary

Sd/-
(S. Chubatoshi Jamir)
Joint Secretary

Dated The 26th October, 1959, MOKOKCHUNG[15]

APPENDIX - THIRTEEN

Prime Minister Atal Bihari Vajpayee's Speech at the Civic Reception in his Honor at the Indira Gandhi Sports Stadium, Kohima on October 28, 2003:

"I am delighted to be with you here this morning.

Ami laga Bhai aru Boyni khan

Aami Nagaland te matiya karune

besi khushi payase

आमि लगा भाई अरु बोयनी खान
आमि नागालैण्ड ते मातिया करुणे
बेसी खुशी पायसे

My dear brothers and sisters, I am indeed happy to be in Nagaland. Thank you.

My hearty greetings to all of you. I also bring you the greetings of all your compatriots from the rest of India.

I am touched by the warmth of your welcome.

This is my first visit to Nagaland after becoming the Prime Minister. I want to express my regrets for not coming here earlier.

From time to time, people from Nagaland have been meeting me. I have kept myself abreast of the situation here. I am as happy as all of you that the developments are moving in a positive direction.

I am convinced that there is an overwhelming desire among Naga people for a permanent peace with honour and dignity. The Central Government has an equally strong desire for permanent peace in Nagaland, based on a lasting solution, with honour and dignity for its people.

It is this mutual desire that has driven the peace process forward. If we continue to work together in an atmosphere of mutual trust, understanding and patience, the day is not far when we reach our goal.

I sincerely thank all the brothers and sisters belonging to different organizations who have contributed to the progress of the peace process. I appreciate the constructive role played by various religious, social groups and NGOs. I thank all of them for their efforts.

Unfortunately, too much blood was shed in Nagaland in the decades gone by. A lot of people suffered. The wheels of development stopped. Mistakes were committed.

Now the time has come to leave the sad chapter of conflict and violence behind us. Rather than remaining tied to the past, we have to take care of the present and look to the future.

This is the time for reconciliation and peace-making. This is also the path that Mahatma Gandhi and Loknayak Jayprakash Narayan wanted us to follow. Both were true friends of Naga people.

It is true that, of all the States in India, Nagaland has a unique history. We are sensitive to this historical fact.

But this uniqueness has in no way diminished the spirit of patriotism among the Naga people. We have the inspiring examples of Patriot Jadunong, who became a martyr, and Rani Gaidinliu. Who can forget that in critical times of war in 1962, 1965 and 1971, Naga underground organizations did not fire on the Indian Army? They showed restraint. I would also like to acknowledge the sacrifices of jawans from Nagaland during the Kargil War.

In times of crisis, all of India becomes one. From Kashmir to Kanyakumari, and from Kutch to Kohima, the same feeling of unity and responsibility runs through.

Nobody can deny that in India's security and development lie the security and development of all of our States, including Nagaland. Similarly, in the peace and development of Nagaland and all other States lies the overall well-being of India.

We have to further strengthen these bonds of solidarity.

My dear Naga sisters and brothers, as we move

closer to permanent peace in Nagaland based on a permanent solution to the issues that have engaged us for the past many decades, I want to assure you on certain counts.

We do not wish to impose any external customs on you. India has a long tradition of tolerating diverse customs and ways of life. You have nothing to fear.

Throughout history, India has been a laboratory of Unity in Diversity to the entire world. India's uniqueness and strength lies in her diversity. Therefore, Nagaland's unique tradition has contributed to India's strength.

I wish to assure you on another score. India is a secular nation, both because of our Constitution and, more importantly, because of our civilisational ethos. As you know, India is home to all the faiths in the world. India has respected and protected all faiths.

Indeed, Christianity came to India -- to the southern State of Kerala -- before it spread to most parts of Europe. And it was a Hindu king who donated land for a church to be built.

We also respect your traditional system of governance. Many tribal representatives tell us, "We have a sound way of managing the affairs of our villages. Why should we always learn from others? Why cannot others learn from us?"

I agree. There are many good things that others

should learn from Nagaland. For example, the practice of broadbased debate and consensual decision-making in your Naga Ho-Hos is the very kernel of democracy. It deserves to be emulated at all levels – from the village level to the global level.

Yesterday your Chief Minister and his colleagues made a presentation on the situation in the State. I would like to commend the State's reform efforts, particularly the communitisation of social service institutions, such as schools and rural health centers. The Centre will fully support such reforms. Yours is indeed a model for other States to follow.

Today Nagaland is a proud and honoured member of the larger Indian Family. This Indian Family may comprise of big States and small, but all are equal. Some States may have a large population and some far less. But all enjoy the same status.

Indeed, our Constitution guarantees that smaller and disadvantaged States get more assistance than others. My Government is especially sensitive to the needs of all Special Category States, including Nagaland.

For example, your Chief Minister came to me sometime back seeking assistance from the Centre to overcome the State's financial crisis. We responded positively. We converted an earlier loan of Rs. 365 crore into a grant.

Our vision is to ensure that no State, no region and no social group in India remains weak and disadvantaged. We are especially keen that our North-Eastern region achieves speedy and all-round development.

Our goal is to remove poverty, unemployment, social disparities and regional imbalances. Our goal is to remove the distance between the more developed and the less developed. In Hindi, I keep saying,

हम दूरी को दूर करना चाहते हैं।
हम दिलों की दूरी को भी दूर करना चाहते हैं।

We want to remove the distance between people, created by geography. That is why, we are improving the air and rail connectivity between the North-East and the rest of India. That is why, we have ushered in a telecom and IT revolution in India.

Today, India's mobile market is the fastest growing in the world. And we said, why should Nagaland be deprived of the fruits of this mobile phone revolution? I am happy that we inaugurated BSNL's mobile phone service in Nagaland yesterday.

We are also minimizing the distance between places through good road connectivity. For the first time since Independence, we are building a world-class four-lane highway network connecting the North and South of India, and the West, East and North-East of India. We are spending Rs. 54,000 crore on this National Highway Development Project.

We are not keeping Nagaland out of this ambitious project. Earlier, this highway network was planned to come up to Silchar. Today I am happy to announce that Kohima will also be connected to this project with a four-lane highway. The Centre will spend Rs. 400 crore on widening this road on National Highway 39. And the work will start next year.

Now, the Government of Nagaland has approached us with proposals to construct some important roads within the State. The Centre will provide Rs. 50 crore for this purpose. However, I have one condition. The roads must be of good quality – much better than the existing roads.

Speaking of roads in Nagaland, I have to say that I had a first-hand experience yesterday. Mother Nature wanted me to take the road journey from Dimapur to Kohima. I was told that, of all the roads in the State, this is the best. If this is the best, it is difficult to imagine how bad is the worst.

I am therefore pleased to announce that the Border Roads Organisation will immediately undertake significant improvement of the Dimapur-Kohima road as part of making it a four-lane highway.

As you know, we have also launched a massive project to connect all the villages in India with good, all-weather roads. We are spending Rs. 60,000 crore on Pradhan Mantri Gram Sadak Yojana, which is the biggest rural infrastructure development since Independence. I would like Nagaland to take full advantage of this project.

All these projects are creating lakhs of new employment opportunities. They are giving a boost to our agriculture, industry and a host of new services. I would like Nagaland to fully benefit from these projects.

Your Chief Minister told me that unemployment among the youth is a major problem in Nagaland. This problem has to be addressed in innovative ways. The nature of employment generation has undergone a change all over the world – including in India. Government jobs cannot be the main source of employment generation. We have to create more and more productive self-employment opportunities.

In this context, I am pleased to announce that the Centre will work closely with the State Government to create 25,000 employment and self-employment opportunities in Nagaland over the next two years. These will be in village industries, tourism, transport, horticulture, fruit-processing and other sectors that best use your strengths and resources. The State Government's Bamboo Mission will be fully supported.

Farmers are the backbone of Indian society. I want to congratulate the farmers of Nagaland for the innovations they have introduced in their traditional jhum cultivation. These innovations need to be further developed and promoted.

I am aware of your amazing bio-diversity – indeed of the entire North-Eastern region. There is a big potential for development of horticulture, floriculture and medicinal plants here. I was very recently in Thailand and was wonderstruck by the beauty and variety of orchids they grow. The flowers and fruits from Thailand – and even countries as far away as Australia and New Zealand – can now be found in the markers of Delhi. Therefore, can we not develop this potential in Nagaland? We can. And we will.

The Centre will lend full support to the speedy and all-round development of Nagaland and the entire North-Eastern region. However, we also need the support of the people, political parties, social organizations, NGOs and governments in this region.

The deepest desire of the people of this region is for peace. Peace is also a precondition for the development of the North-East. Without peace, there can be no private sector investment and no development. Without development, there can be no employment.

I therefore appeal to the misguided organisations in this region, which have taken to the path of extremism and violence, to shun that path. The Centre is willing to have talks with all those who are ready to give up the gun culture, and take to the culture of dialogue and democracy.

There is no issue, which cannot be resolved through sufficiently long and patient dialogue. Our experience in Nagaland is showing this.

The need for peace has another side to it in the North-East. Even issues between tribes and organizations should be resolved peacefully through dialogue. Violent rivalries can have no place in our vision of a progressive, peaceful and prosperous Nagaland, in which every tribe benefits and no one is left behind.

My second appeal is to all those who are a part of the government and administration at different levels. The under-development of the North-Eastern region is not necessarily on account of shortage of funds. However, funds must be used judiciously. Corruption is an enemy of development.

There should be proper accountability – both at the political and bureaucratic levels. Projects should be completed on time. Otherwise, we end up spending several times more than the originally planned amount. We also lose valuable time. Take the case of this stadium itself, which I am inaugurating. This is your State. You should take responsibility for its development.

No citizen or businessman in the State should feel unsafe and intimidated. The rule of law should be respected.

Development of the North-East sometimes suffers from another drawback. Often, government departments and agencies draw up plans and implement programmes without adequate participation of the people. Schemes are formulated in a uniform manner for everybody without taking into account their relevance to local needs and conditions.

Here I am reminded of the story of a king who once went on a tour of a province in his kingdom. The place was hot and he came across children who were going to school barefoot and with their heads unprotected. He ordered his officers to make sure that every child got a pair of shoes and a cap. "Jee huzoor," said the officers. After a few weeks, they sent a consignment from the capital containing shoes and caps. On a subsequent visit to the same province, the king saw that only a small number of children were wearing them.

He asked the officers accompanying him why this was so. They replied, "Your majesty, we promptly implemented your order and dispatched the required quantity of goods from the capital." The king then turned to the headmaster of the school and posed the same question.

The headmaster said, "Your Majesty, the officers are right. They did send us the required number of shoes and caps, but all of them were of the same size. They probably expected that, instead of changing the size of the shoes and caps to fit the children's feet and head, the children should change the size of their feet and head to fit what they had so generously sent us."

The people should have a say in what kind of development they want. We should harmonise our national priorities, State priorities and local priorities through constant dialogue.

Today there are coalition governments both in Kohima and in New Delhi. The National Democratic Alliance has as many as two dozen parties. Many of them are small parties, but they have an equal place in the NDA. We respect them. Our alliance has shown that regional aspirations can be harmonized with a strong national outlook. In this sense, the NDA is a mini-India in the political field.

Our alliance has also shown that a coalition government at the Centre can be stable. We have not only provided stability; we have also provided dynamism to India's development. India's prestige has risen all over the world. Among other things, this is reflected in India's growing ties with ASEAN countries.

I give my best wishes to the Government of the Democratic Alliance in Nagaland. I would like it to work as a model of good governance and responsible governance for all other States in the North-East. I would also like to thank the people of Nagaland for their support to the BJP, which is now a part of the ruling coalition.

In a democracy, there will always be some parties in power and others in the opposition. Some will win and others will lose. This process will continue. But whether a party is in power or in the opposition, all should work together for the common good of the State and its people.

In this, we should learn from the traditional democratic practice of village councils in Nagaland.

With these words, I conclude my speech. I thank you for this very warm reception. My best wishes to all of you. My best wishes to the peace process. I assure you that you will find a trustworthy partner in my Government in reaching the cherished goal of lasting peace in Nagaland with dignity and honour for its people.

Aami khan sob milikina

Nagaland tu bhal korikena bo nabo

आमि खान सोव मिलिकिना
नागालैण्ड तु भाल कोरिकेना बो नाबो।

Let us together build a New Nagaland. Dhanyabaad.

Thank you".

1. http://www.britannica.com/topic/sovereignty#body -1.
2. http://www.britannica.com/topic/sovereignty#body -2.
3. http://www.britannica.com/topic/sovereignty#body -3.
4. http://www.britannica.com/topic/sovereignty#body -4.
5. http://www.britannica.com/topic/sovereignty#body -5.
6. http://www.britannica.com/topic/sovereignty#body -6.
7. https://www.academia.edu/2763366/Shared_Sover eignty_and_the_European_Union_The_Transition_t o_Post-Westphalian_Sovereignty#body-1.
8. https://www.academia.edu/2763366/Shared_Sover eignty_and_the_European_Union_The_Transition_t o_Post-Westphalian_Sovereignty#body-2
9. https://www.marxists.org/archive/guevara/1960/03 /20.htm
10. http://www.yourarticlelibrary.com/indian-constitution/7-main-federal-features-of-the-indian-constitution/24924/#body-1.
11. http://www.yourarticlelibrary.com/indian-constitution/7-main-federal-features-of-the-indian-constitution/24924/#body-2.
12. http://www.yourarticlelibrary.com/indian-constitution/7-main-federal-features-of-the-indian-constitution/24924/#body-3.
13. http://www.yourarticlelibrary.com/indian-constitution/7-main-federal-features-of-the-indian-constitution/24924/#body-4.

14. http://www.yourarticlelibrary.com/indian-constitution/7-main-federal-features-of-the-indian-constitution/24924/#body-5.
15. Naga People Convention and 16-Point Agreement by Dr SC Jamir, 2011, Page - 54

ABOUT THE AUTHOR

Oken Jeet Sandham began his career with the Weekly Journal, Kohima as early as in 1987, later rechristened it as The Nagaland Journal. He worked with The Statesman from 1998 to 2000 before joining the Hindustan Times till 2001 as 'Stringer." He writes regularly on various issues –politics, socio-economy, sports, governance, insurgency, tourism, culture, etc. His writings have been widely published and numbers of his activities have also been published in various magazines around the world. He was Editor of The Northeast Herald, now defunct. He is currently the Editor of the North East Press Service (NEPS), www.nepsnews.in, an Independent News Agency published from Kohima, Nagaland. He has been in martial arts activities particularly Muaythai for the last nearly three decades and has widely traveled. He was Vice Chairman of Development Commission of the International Federation of Muaythai Amateur (IFMA), www.ifmamuaythai.org, Bangkok, Thailand and was also Executive Member of the Federation of Amateur Muaythai of Asia (FAMA), Singapore. He has led Indian Muaythai Teams to a number of

World Muaythai Championships, Seminars, Conventions, and Workshops. He led the Indian Muaythai Team to the 13th Bangkok Asian Games 1998 and was Jury in the 24th SEA Games 2007 at Korat, Thailand. He also led Indian Muaythai Team in the World Sports for All Games 2008 at Busan, South Korea. He is currently the President of Muaythai Federation of India (MFI) and K-1 Federation of India (K-1FI). He is the sole Representative of World Muaythai Federation (WMF). He served as Secretary of the prestigious Lions Club of Kohima from 2010 to 2015.